ༀ་མ་ཎི་པ་དྨེ་ཧཱུྃ

THE WORLD OF THE
DALAI LAMA

May all sentient beings have happiness and the causes of happiness.

May all sentient beings be free from suffering and the causes of suffering.

May all sentient beings never be separated from the happiness that knows no suffering.

May all sentient beings abide in equanimity, free from attachment

and anger that hold some close and others distant.

THE WORLD OF THE
DALAI LAMA

An Inside Look at His Life,
His People, and His Vision

~

Gill Farrer-Halls

A publication supported by
THE KERN FOUNDATION

Quest Books
Theosophical Publishing House

Wheaton, Illinois ♦ Chennai (Madras), India

For additional information write to:
The Theosophical Publishing House

P. O. Box 270

Wheaton, IL 60189-0270

A publication of the Theosophical Publishing House,
a department of the Theosophical Society in America

Designed and edited by
The Bridgewater Book Company Ltd

Picture research by Jane Moore

Library of Congress Cataloging-in-Publication Data

Farrer-Halls, Gill.
    The world of the Dalai Lama: an inside look at his life, his people,
and his vision/Gill Farrer-Halls. – 1st Quest ed.
        p. cm.
    "Quest books."
    ISBN 0-8356-0768-2
    1. Bstan-'dzin-rgya-mtsho, Dalai Lama XIV, 1935– 2. Dalai lamas
    –Biography. 3. Tibet (China)–Civilization. 4. Buddhism–Doctrines.
    5. Tibet (China)–Politics and government–1951– 6. Tibet
    (China)–Religion.   I. Title
    BQ7935.B777F37   1998
    294.3'923'092–dc21
    [B]   97-37417
                                                           CIP

    ISBN 0-8356-0768-2

Printed in Hong Kong

QUEST BOOKS are published by
The Theosophical Society in America,
Wheaton, Illinois 60189–0270,
a branch of a world organization dedicated to the promotion of the unity of humanity and the encouragement
of the study of religion, philosophy, and science, to the
end that we may better understand ourselves and our
place in the universe. The Society stands for complete
freedom of individual search and belief.
For further information about its activities,
write or call 1–800–669–1571, or consult its Web page;
http://www.theosophical.org

The Theosophical Publishing House
is aided by the generous support of
THE KERN FOUNDATION,
a trust established by Herbert A. Kern
and dedicated to Theosophical education.

Author's Acknowledgments
I would like to thank Martine Batchelor and Carol Tonkinson for suggesting I write this book, Debbie Thorpe, my
editor at Godsfield Press, and Brenda Rosen, editor at Quest Books, and Peter Bridgewater and Caroline Earle at the
Bridgewater Book Company. I would also like to thank Robbie Barnett at Tibet Information Network and
Robyn Brentano for their help and information. Special thanks to Stephen Batchelor for advice and
encouragement throughout, and Jane Moore for her professional work, friendship and support.

Frontispiece: People waiting to greet the Dalai Lama at Kalachakra initiation in Spiti, northern India, 1996
Title page: The Dalai Lama meditating at home in Dharamsala
Page 5: Mani stone from Dat village, Rupshu, Zanskar

CONTENTS

~

Introduction

Reflecting upon the title of this book, I realize it could just as well be called The Worlds of the Dalai Lama. *His life has straddled two very different worlds: the almost medieval Old Tibet of his childhood, isolated and infused with religion; and the modern world of his current life. His is a unique experience given the lifestyle of his office, and he is one of only a few who have such a privileged overview of both ways of life.*

Far right: Prayer flags overlooking Samye Monastery, Tibet

Below: The Dalai Lama meditating at home in Dharamsala

The phrase "Old Tibet" conjures up particular visions and ideas, some of which are realistic while others tap into the myths that abound around this mountain kingdom. Sometimes known as Shangri-la, the last country to be touched by the modern world, Tibet is situated high in the Himalayas. Its borders were once largely inaccessible to all but the most intrepid and determined visitors who were prepared to hike over potentially dangerous mountain passes and circumvent the official line regarding foreign visitors. But for those who risked the perilous journey, the reward was encountering an ancient civilization that had hardly changed over the centuries.

Old Tibet was about two-thirds monastic, with many monasteries and nunneries, some housing thousands of monks. Most families sent at least one child to take orders. This was not a strictly vocational path, nor were all the monks and nuns intelligent and immersed in religious studies, but being a monastic provided a traditional way of life. Lay people either lived in the few large towns and numerous small villages or were wandering nomads who grazed their livestock. Buddhism was integral to their lifestyles too, and many lay people were deeply religious.

Tibetans are a hardy people since the climate can be harsh and inhospitable. Old Tibet lacked all but the most basic sanitation, and many people had no access to nonmonastic education. Tibetan medicine, though relatively sophisticated and effective, was also not widely available to ordinary folk. Though most people were committed to the Buddhist principles of peace and nonviolence, some examples of early Tibetan history are surprisingly bloodthirsty and feature tales of political coups and murderous intrigues. However, most people in this mountain kingdom at the turn of the century were content with their lot, living with few changes as their ancestors had always lived and largely at peace and harmony with themselves and with their environment. This was the world into which the 14th Dalai Lama was born, one that has since disappeared forever.

Today the Dalai Lama lives in Dharamsala, north India, in the foothills of the Himalayas, along with the majority of Tibetans in exile. The sound of Tibetan

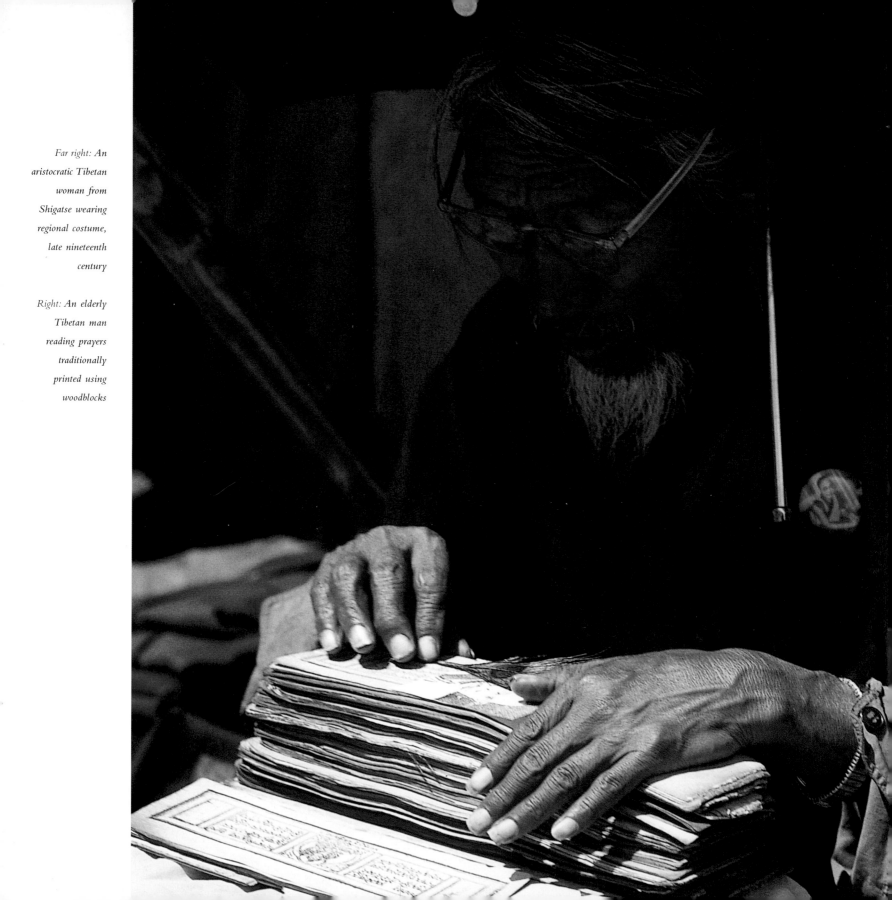

Top left: Tibetan nomad children wearing sheepskin coats called chubas

Below left: A nomad mother and child in Amdo (now a Chinese province) holding a picture of the Dalai Lama given by a foreign traveler; such pictures are often forbidden by the Chinese authorities

horns heralding Buddhist ceremonies drifts through the mountain air, and prayer flags flutter in the wind as they have always done. Along the main streets are small shops that sell traditional Tibetan clothes, religious artifacts, and jewelry alongside literature, posters, and flags crying out for a free Tibet. Although, like neighboring Indian towns, things appear a little shabby to the Western tourist, there is a sense of bustling prosperity. However, behind the main thoroughfares is another story. Here are little shantytowns made up of poor, tin-roof shacks, where many of the people who escape from Tibet and come over the mountains to freedom, unable to carry their many possessions, end up living.

The Dalai Lama's residence is in a pleasant compound near the main temple, but it is modest for a man who is the leader of a government, albeit in exile, and a renowned international figure. Much of the time he is away fulfilling the many requests for Buddhist teachings, participating in conferences, and tirelessly repeating his message of peace, love, and compassion in public forums all over the world. When he is at home there is a constant stream of visitors, all of whom are greeted with the same humorous warmth, whether the visitor is a foreign dignitary or simply one of the many ordinary people who wish to have a brief meeting with him.

Increasingly during his tours, he speaks of the tragedy that his people are suffering, either in exile or in Tibet living under the oppression of the Chinese regime. During his U.K. visit in 1996, he voiced his concern with great sadness that a unique culture was in danger of being destroyed forever. Yet no major foreign government formally recognizes the Tibetan government in exile.

Winning the Nobel Peace Prize in 1989 gave international recognition to the Dalai Lama's peaceful methods for trying to resolve the Chinese occupation of Tibet. He continues to attempt to negotiate with the Chinese government, despite receiving no encouragement from them, and always remains open to dialog. Sometimes he appears sad, almost desperate, in his attempts to gain help for his people. Yet whenever the Dalai Lama gives Buddhist teachings, he is obviously happy to be able to share the wisdom of Buddhism, and during his public talks he is often very funny as well as inspiring.

The Dalai Lama plays many roles: spiritual and political leader of the Tibetans, Buddhist teacher, spokesperson for peace, interfaith proponent, and ambassador for his people and their beleaguered country. Yet he frequently describes himself as a simple Buddhist monk, and this is really what he is happiest being. It is this simplicity that allows him to synthesize his other roles and move between them with such ease and also the quality that endears him to people throughout the world.

As a member of a video crew that has filmed the Dalai Lama on several occasions, I have had the precious opportunity to be near him. I have never failed to be impressed by his openness and delight at meeting people, as well as by how everyone who encounters him is moved, often considerably. Indeed, his Tibetan nickname is "Kundun," which means "The Presence," and even hardened journalists who are purported to have "seen it all" are surprised at their reactions to this man. *The World of the Dalai Lama* is a tribute to His Holiness the Dalai Lama. In writing it, I hope to open up the world of the Dalai Lama to all who read it.

Top right:

A stupa at Drigung Monastery, 60 miles (100 kilometers) northeast of Lhasa, containing relics of the founder Jigten Gonpo

Below center:

A young Khampa girl wearing red silk braided into her hair, along with pieces of turquoise and coral

Below right:

A young Tibetan girl sitting next to prayer flags on a mountain pass

Old Tibet

Map of Old Tibet showing major mountain ranges, surrounding countries, largest monasteries and towns.

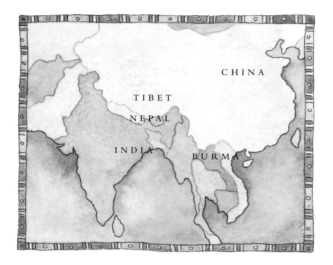

KEY

❖	*largest monasteries*
●	*towns/cities*
▲	*mountains*
	1914 border

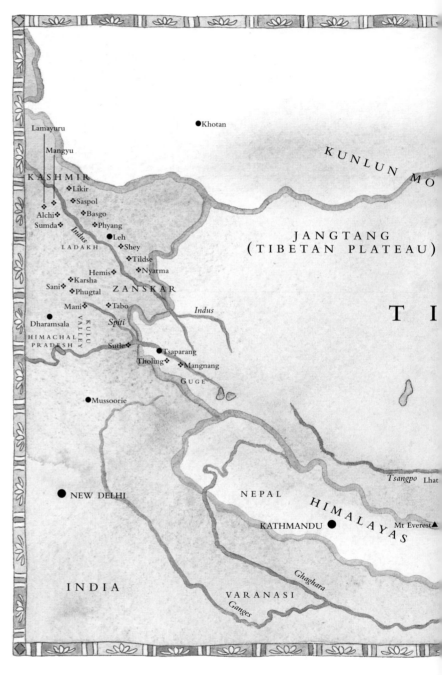

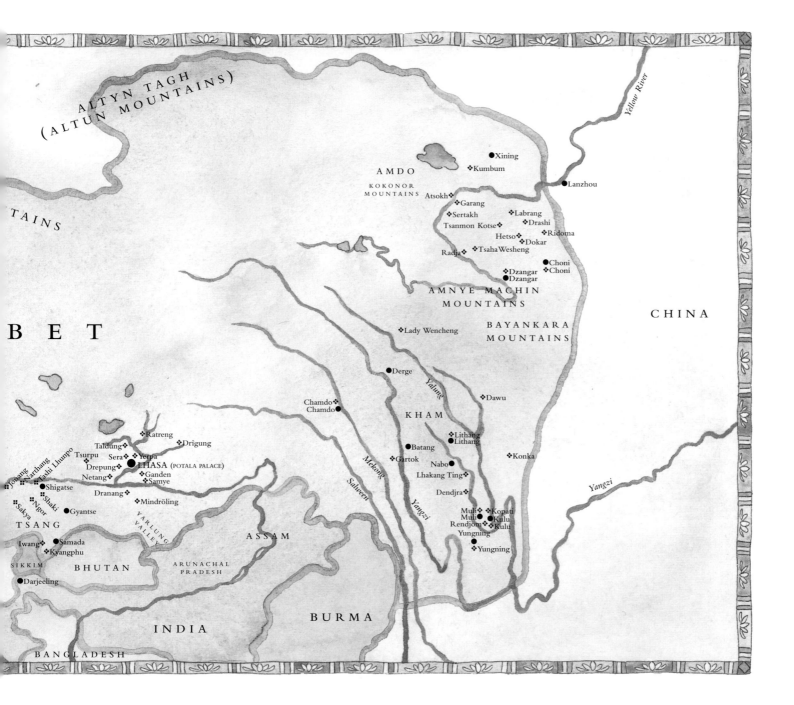

ALTYN TAGH
(ALTUN MOUNTAINS)

AMDO

KOKONOR
MOUNTAINS

●Xining
❖Kumbum

Lanzhou●

Yellow River

Atsokh❖
❖Garang
❖Sertakh   ❖Labrang
Tsanmon Kotse❖   ❖Drashi
            Hetso❖   ❖Ridoma
                ❖Dokar
Radja❖   ❖TsahaWesheng

●Choni
❖Choni

❖Dzangar
●Dzangar

AMNYE MACHIN
MOUNTAINS

CHINA

❖Lady Wencheng   BAYANKARA
MOUNTAINS

B E T

TAINS

●Derge

Yalung

❖Dawu

Chamdo❖
Chamdo●

KHAM

❖Lithang
●Lithang

●Konka

❖Ratreng
Taldüng❖   ❖Drigung
Tsurpu❖   ❖Yerpa
Sera❖
Drepung❖   ●LHASA (POTALA PALACE)
Netang❖   ❖Ganden
    ❖Samye
Dranang❖
    ❖Mindröling

●Batang
❖Gartok   Nabo●
        Lhakang Ting❖

Dendjra❖

Mekong

Salween

Yangzi

Yangzi

Yangzi

Muli❖ ❖Kopari
Muli● ❖Kulu
Rendjöm❖ ●Kulu
    Yungning
    ❖Yungning
    ●Yungning

Jobang
Narthang
Tashi Lhunpo
●Shigatse
❖Shaki
Sakya❖ ❖Ngor
Iwang❖
T S A N G ●Gyantse
    ●Samada
    ❖Kyangphu

YARLUNG
VALLEY

ASSAM

SIKKIM
BHUTAN   ARUNACHAL
            PRADESH

●Darjeeling

I N D I A

B U R M A

BANGLADESH

part one
~
TIBET

1
~
Tibet before the Chinese Invasion

The old Tibet was not perfect. Yet at the same time it is true to say that our way of life was something quite remarkable. Certainly there was much that was worth preserving that is now lost forever.

14TH DALAI LAMA

Previous pages: Clockwise from left: crowds enjoying the Shoton Festival at Drepung Monastery; two nomad women; a nomad girl wearing a coral and turquoise headdress

Right: Khampa man with a yak at Hebu, near Samye

ibet is the world's highest country, with an average altitude of 15,000 feet (4,572 meters). It is divided into three main provinces: Kham, Amdo, and U-Tsang, the latter containing the capital, Lhasa. The Tibetan plateau is ringed by mountains, with the famous Himalayas to the south, and other ranges forming an almost unbroken natural barrier, except in the northeast. This geographical fact helps to explain why Tibet's culture was able to remain almost unchanged for such a long time.

THE TIBETAN WAY OF LIFE
Tibet is a country of devastating beauty and great harshness, with spectacular mountains, vast, arid plains in the center sloping down to fertile plains and valleys, and huge forests. This dual nature is reflected in the Tibetan character, which is both fierce and gentle. Their ferocity, which ensures survival in a tough climate is tempered by the Buddhist reverence for all living beings, which is expressed with compassion and wisdom. Sparsely populated – a country roughly the size of Western Europe inhabited by only seven million people – and with a conservative feudal system, life continued naturally with little outside influence.

With the establishment of Buddhism in the eighth century, there gradually evolved huge monasteries, which eventually became home to a quarter of the male population. A less significant number of nunneries also existed. Like their Western counterparts, the monasteries were centers of learning and culture as well as of religious pursuits. Tibetan monks had the opportunity to study medicine and astrology, art and sculpture, literature and poetry. All studies were based on the tenets of Buddhism, which formed the core of monastic education, such as the belief that all things are impermanent and subject to change, thus causing the inherent nature of existence to be unsatisfactory.

Existing alongside learned knowledge were the rituals, prayers, and ceremonies of Tibetan Buddhism.

In Tibet, the loftiest land on earth, even valleys
run higher than the summit of any mountain
in Europe, Canada, or the United States.

SIR CHARLES BELL

These are colorful, complex, and involve chanting mantras (sacred sounds), reciting texts and prayers, performing mudras (symbolic hand gestures), and lama dances in which the proponents act out metaphysical battles with demons through ritual movement. There were also great, solitary, yogic adepts, who would spend many years practicing asceticism and meditation in isolated caves. After realizing profound truths about existence, they might attract disciples who would request teachings.

Above: Samye Monastery, founded by Trisong Detsen in the eighth century, the first Buddhist monastery in Tibet

The head of a monastery was called a lama – literally, "spiritual teacher" – and there would be several lamas in the monastic hierarchy. There were also the mundane aspects of existence to take care of, and monks who were not particularly gifted at deep spiritual study or art might be cooks or gardeners, though, of course, spending part of the day performing religious practices. The monasteries were self-contained units catering for all the monks' needs, both spiritual and physical. They were supported by the lay society

through a system of taxation, which was sometimes repressive and impeded social and economic mobility. However, the lay people largely accepted this imposition quite cheerfully, and in return for material support, the monks provided religious advice, spiritual support, ceremonies, and prayers to mark deaths and other major events.

Alongside the religious hierarchy, there existed also an aristocracy. Through the centuries there had been various kings and dynasties, which stabilized into a noble elite, some of whose members could trace their ancestry back to the Yarlung kings of the first recorded royal dynasty. They wore gorgeous clothes of embroidered silk brocade, not unlike the sumptuous ceremonial robes of the high lamas, and magnificent, often heavy, jewelry worn by the nobles denoted their role in society. This was no idle opulence, however, since the aristocracy, together with the religious hierarchy, ruled the country.

What a marvelous spectacle it is to see a cavalcade of high Tibetan officials in their beautiful Chinese brocades, golden and blue, mounted on their shaggy ponies and mules, coming over the crest of a pass and descending toward you, lit by the brilliant Tibetan sunshine in a cloudless sky.

SIR CHARLES BELL

In return for the large estates on which they lived, the nobility performed governmental services. Each administrative job was headed by both a monk and a member of the nobility. This prevented either side from developing too much power and was a useful check on corruption. This successful system functioned from the inauguration of government under the Dalai Lamas to 1959. Their intimacy with the

religious hierarchy also prevented the nobility from degenerating into decadence, since all its members maintained a family shrine room and kept a retinue of monks who performed daily prayers and rituals.

The nobility still enjoyed a privileged role and boasted many fine possessions, often rare in Tibet and symbolic of successful trading ventures. Parties and picnics that frequently lasted a few days at a time were not uncommon in the summer. These were held in beautiful and well-kept gardens that contained a large variety of flowers and plants, together with peacocks and other forms of wildlife. Chang – Tibetan beer made of fermented barley – was drunk at such occasions. But the moderating influence of the Dharma (the Buddhist teachings) kept the enjoyment of privilege and luxury among the nobility from excess.

The remainder of the population were mostly nomadic farmers and traders who lived in small settlements or in the few larger towns. Regional variations, such as distinctive styles of dress and dialect, were largely due to the vastness of the country; parts of Tibet were virtually uninhabited, thereby hindering frequent communication with distant neighbors. The highest lands were inhabited by nomads who lived in tents and wandered between pastures with huge herds of yaks and sheep, according to the season. Freedom-loving and independent, they kept themselves isolated, making only a couple of trips to town each year to trade meat, cheese, and hides for grain, tea, and guns.

In the lower, fertile valleys the farmers lived mostly in small settlements and grew barley, the staple crop and food of Tibet. Barley was roasted and ground into tsampa (barley flour), which was mixed into large bowls of Tibetan tea made with butter and salt, and formed the main national meal. These agricultural

people were in greater thrall to the neighboring monastery and nobleman's estate than their nomadic cousins, and paying taxes of labor, goods, and money was the accepted way of life from which there was virtually no escape.

> *With the tea is mixed butter and a kind of soda which is found as a white powder on the margins of lakes, and mainly on the highlands of northern and western Tibet. The people drink from twenty to fifty cups a day of ordinary tea-cup size. Europeans dislike it intensely, but it is not unwholesome.*
>
> SIR CHARLES BELL

Trade, however, could provide a way out, both geographically and economically. Caravans of traders

Above: A view of the village of Shol at the foot of the Potala, photographed here in 1954. The village has now been almost obliterated

departed each fall after the harvest, some traveling within the country, others making the long trip to India, China, or Mongolia. They traded surplus food, salt, gold, medicinal herbs, wool, and hides for tea, silver, silk, tools, tobacco, and other luxury foreign items. These caravans might be attacked by bandits unless they were large and well defended, and the journey was often perilous. Successful traders, however, did well and some chose not to return.

Not only material goods were exchanged. The great trade routes also facilitated cultural and religious communication: sacred texts were introduced, and teachers from India visited Tibet, while some Tibetan translators would spend years working and studying at the great Indian teaching monasteries before returning home carrying their translated texts. Such an exchange of ideas helped Buddhism in Tibet to develop its own unique practices, as Buddhism gradually declined in India.

Above: Ranee Taring, a famous aristocrat of the 1930s

LHASA

People from all walks of life tended to gravitate to Lhasa at some point in their lives. Not only was it the capital city offering access to a variety of goods not easily found elsewhere, where people could see Tibetan operas and other entertainments, but Lhasa also housed many of the most revered temples and was furthermore home to the Dalai Lama. Many people from the far-flung regions of Tibet would travel for weeks, sometimes months, to make a pilgrimage to the holy city, a major event in their lives.

Built next to the Otang Lake in U-Tsang province, the town was originally called Rasa, a word that reflects the sound of the wind moving the water. Songtsen Gampo, who ruled for twenty years during the seventh century, first called the city Lhasa, meaning "Ground of the Gods," and moved his capital there from Yarlung. In Lhasa he also built Tibet's most sacred temple – the Jokhang – which was further enhanced by the 5th Dalai Lama and contained many old and sacred statues.

Pilgrims would circumambulate the Jokhang on the Barkor, a series of streets immediately surrounding the temple. They would often work their way around by prostrating themselves full length on the ground, moving forward one body length, and then repeating the procedure, thus earning themselves much spiritual merit. Others would walk while counting out their recitations of mantras with a string of prayer beads called a mala, or while twirling prayer wheels – circular metal wheels mounted on a wooden handle containing prayers printed by woodblocks on paper. Along the streets were market stalls selling a wide variety of goods, and traders mingled freely with those making their religious devotions.

Left: Women gathering the grain harvest in Nyemu, near Shigatse, in western Tibet

On a hill to the west of the main city lies the Potala. Built by the 5th Dalai Lama, this imposing and beautiful palace has been home to all subsequent Dalai Lamas. As well as the Dalai Lama's personal quarters, the Potala contained several chapels, shrines, and halls built for religious and governmental purposes. At about the

Above: One of the foremost Nyingma lamas, the late Dilgo Khyentse Rinpoche

time of the 8th Dalai Lama, it became the Dalai Lama's winter quarters, the Norbulingka (The Jewel Park) becoming his residence for the summer. Many of Tibet's famous monasteries were situated nearby, including the so-called "Great Three" of Ganden, Drepung, and Sera.

Lhasa was a thriving ancient city, the seat of government, a place of pilgrimage, and the hub of Tibetan society. Monks, traders, nobles, pilgrims, beggars, children, and animals mingled freely in the bustling streets. Huge crowds would gather for such major religious festivals as the Monlam, or "Prayer Festival," in the early spring. These were joyous occasions, with celebrations and festivities intermingled with religious ceremony. Huge, colorful processions would parade along the streets carrying holy statues, as the smell of incense and butter lamps perfumed the air.

The last day of the Monlam festival was given over to outdoor activities. Firstly, a large statue of Maitreya, the Buddha to come, would lead a procession round the perimeter of the old city… Soon after the statue had completed its circuit, there would be a general commotion as people turned their attention to sporting activities. These were great fun and involved both horse races and running races for members of the public.

14TH DALAI LAMA

This ancient feudalistic culture was not without its drawbacks, however. Outside of the monasteries there was little formal education; sanitation and hygiene were poor; and there was scant opportunity to change one's station in life. Political intrigue and power struggles were rife, particularly during the weak periods between Dalai Lamas when a regent would rule until the new incarnation came of age. Lhasa had a prison, and penalties for crimes could be brutal. Bandits, as well as wild animals, would attack the unwary traveler, and the harsh climate and delicate ecostructure made farming a risky business.

Yet people prospered within the limits of the system. There were no major famines, and most people were happy with their station. Because the majority of families sent at least one child to a monastery, religion was an integral part of life; it also provided a way of life and a living for about a quarter of the population. The spirit of Buddhism, with its emphasis on compassion, reverence for life, and tolerance, permeated everything, and the "last Shangri-la," though not a paradise, was a contented country.

Main picture: A yak caravan laden with baggage approaching Mount Everest

Left: Coolies carrying bundles of tea weighing around 300 pounds (136 kilograms) from China to Tibet, 1908

OLD TIBET

Tibet is bordered by two large countries, India and China, and several smaller ones, including Mongolia, to whose people Tibetans are racially similar. Tibet was originally occupied by small tribes who continuously battled for supremacy, until their first main empire developed with the appearance of Nyatri Tsenpo in about 500 B.C.E. Legend has it that he fell from the skies, but even if he arrived more conventionally, he is still credited with founding the Yarlung Dynasty.

Until the reign of the 28th Yarlung king, Lhatotori, in the fourth century, the rulers had all followed the animistic Bon religion. At this time another legend states that Buddhist scriptures fell from the sky and conveniently landed at the king's court where they were well received. This started a long battle between Bon and Buddhism. In the seventh century Songtsen Gampo strengthened the Buddhist position by marrying both a Chinese and a Nepalese wife who brought with them precious statues from their respective Buddhist countries, and the devout practice of the wives stimulated an interest in Buddhism.

In the eighth century Trisong Detsen consolidated Buddhism in Tibet by inviting Padmasambhava, a great Indian tantric yogi, to subdue the local demons hostile to Buddhism. There was a huge debate and display of magical feats between Padmasambhava and the highest Bon priests; Padmasambhava won spectacularly, which encouraged the Buddhist teachings to spread widely among the populace. However, in the ninth century, Buddhism was violently repressed by King Langdarma, a staunch Bon supporter. The subsequent assassination of Langdarma by an irate Buddhist monk then initiated the demise of the great Yarlung Dynasty.

From India she [Tibet] has received Buddhism, which she has modified to suit her own instincts thereby evolving a strong national religion, the most precious of all her possessions.

SIR CHARLES BELL

Various small principalities then arose. Some in western Tibet followed Buddhism, while some in central Tibet reverted to Bon. In the eleventh century Buddhism flowered anew with the arrival of the great Indian guru Atisha and the Indian teacher Naropa, as well as Marpa, who taught Tibet's most famous yogic "saint" Milarepa. Known as the "Second Dissemination of the Doctrine in Tibet," this period became a Buddhist renaissance of learning, translation, and sacred art. However, at the beginning of the thirteenth century, the notorious and brutal Genghis Khan conquered central Asia. When his envoys arrived in Tibet from Mongolian-dominated China, the Tibetans yielded, hoping to avoid further interference.

Below: Ministers of the Tibetan government prior to the Chinese invasion

Yet, Tibet's failure to keep up the promised payments to Mongolia resulted in its invasion several years later by the grandson of Genghis Khan. After a display of strength involving sacking a major monastery and slaughtering many of the monks, Godan Khan then ironically but diplomatically forged links with one of the traditions of the Tibetan religious hierarchies, aware of its potential political power as much as its religious prestige. The deal was struck with Sakya Pandita, head of the Sakyas, which infuriated the heads of the other traditions, since the khan made the Sakya Pandita regent of Tibet. This gave spiritual guidance to the Mongol leaders and political power to the Sakyas inside Tibet, though the country remained under the Mongol overlord. This situation lasted about a century.

The notion of "patron-priest" was a conveniently ambiguous one that in traditional Asian political relations could work to the advantage of both parties without either of them feeling to be the underdog. To the politically minded Mongols and Manchus, the patron naturally held a superior position to that of the priest. But to the religiously minded Tibetans, the priest held the real and higher power…

STEPHEN BATCHELOR

As Mongolian power waned, the nationalist leader Jangchub Gyeltsen overthrew the Sakya regent and became ruler of Tibet in 1354. When the indigenous Ming Chinese took over from the Mongols in China several years later, the Tibetans chose to forget their "priest-patron" relationship, and Tibet was independent for the next three hundred years. During this period, it was the Kagyus who ruled, and the other traditions continued to jostle for power.

Back home in Mongolia, Altan Khan, a more benign descendant of Genghis, continued to watch Tibet with interest. He was attracted by the newly arisen Geluk, or reform, school, which had been started by Tsongkhapa in the latter half of the fourteenth century. The khan arranged a meeting with Sonam Gyatso (born in 1543), then the leader of the Gelukpas, and was so impressed by this religious man that he gave him the title of Dalai Lama, and also retrospectively conferred it upon his two predecessors. This was the establishment of the Dalai Lama lineage, which endures to this day.

However, the other traditions and powerful local rulers felt threatened by this Gelukpa–Mongol alliance and the 4th Dalai Lama was killed in a coup in 1616. The Mongolians, still supporting the Gelukpas, invaded Tibet, put down the uprising, and firmly instated the 5th Dalai Lama, who, for the first time in Tibet, had complete control, both secular and religious.

Above: The ruins of Tholing in the ancient kingdom of Guge, western Tibet

Right: The Potala Palace in Lhasa, built by the 5th Dalai Lama and home to the Dalai Lamas since the seventeenth century

Known as the "Great Fifth," he ruled wisely and brought a sense of national unity to the country.

The 6th Dalai Lama was an unsuitable ruler, preferring to write poetry and indulge in love affairs. This brought political instability once again, and the powerful Chinese emperor, K'ang Hsi, encouraged the Mongolian prince, Lhabzang Khan, to invade Tibet and replace the 6th Dalai Lama's regent, who in effect was ruling the country, in order to regain stability. This was successful, and the khan offered Tibet in tribute to the Chinese emperor. Another group of Mongols, the Dzungars, who had been allies of the murdered regent, then killed Lhabzang Khan in yet another coup.

Emperor K'ang Hsi put down this rebellion swiftly and instated the young 7th Dalai Lama in 1720. In 1721 he declared Tibet to be a protectorate of China, but Chinese intervention was only necessary on one further occasion: in 1792, when they helped the Tibetans to evict an invasion by the Nepalese. From this time onward the relationship between Tibet and China became a formality. Several Dalai Lamas and regents then ruled more or less peacefully for a century or so, and the only major change that was made during the nineteenth century was the closure of the borders to foreigners, thus creating an isolated and religious country.

RECENT HISTORY

It may happen that here in the center of Tibet the religion and the secular administration may be attacked both from the outside and from the inside... All beings will be sunk in great hardship and in overpowering fear; the days and nights will drag on slowly in suffering.

13TH DALAI LAMA

Tubten Gyatso, the 13th Dalai Lama and the immediate predecessor of the current 14th Dalai Lama, was the head of Tibet as the world entered the twentieth century. He was a strong ruler and became increasingly aware of the precarious status of his country, particularly when he was forced into exile twice during his reign. First, in 1904 when an uninvited British expedition, led by Colonel Francis Younghusband, was sent from India, then a British colony, causing Tubten Gyatso to flee to Mongolia. Ostensibly worried about Russian intervention, the British also secured trade deals, but most important of all, they demonstrated the insubstantial relationship between China and Tibet.

This partly prompted a Manchu Chinese invasion in 1910, which tried to make Tibet a province of China. The 13th Dalai Lama was obliged to flee once again, this time ironically to British India. The Manchus ruled only briefly, being evicted by the Tibetans a year later, when their own country was experiencing the turmoil of revolution. The 13th Dalai Lama then returned from exile and announced the independence of Tibet.

China, however, made claims not only on Tibet but also on Mongolia, Manchuria, and Xinjiang as its provinces. Unable at this time actually to occupy these territories, the Chinese still posed a real threat to Tibetan sovereignty. This prompted the British to arrange the Simla Convention in 1914 between themselves, the Tibetans, and the Chinese. The purpose was to clarify the relationship between the three countries, but since the situation was somewhat murky and complex, the meeting dragged on for six months.

At the conclusion, documents were prepared that proposed that Tibet was an autonomous state but under the suzerainty of China. In practical terms, this would have allowed the Tibetans complete freedom within their own borders, while deferring to China in matters of foreign policy. The Tibetans and the British wanted to sign and make this position official, but the Chinese refused to accept this arrangement and in 1950 invaded Tibet to "reunite them [Tibetans] with the motherland." Tibet still remains an occupied country today.

BON

Bon was the indigenous animistic religion of Tibet before Buddhism and, although largely assimilated into the newer religion, still exists today.

Bon was based largely on worship of the forces of nature. But it was more than mere nature worship; it was strongly organized and ... Buddhism succeeded only by compromising with Bon, adopting many of its ideas.

SIR CHARLES BELL

Bon involved the worship of good spirits, the propitiation of demons, and to achieve these it also included animal sacrifice.

Tibetans divide it into White Bon and Black Bon. The White Bon have now become almost like the Buddhists, the differences between them not being reckoned as vital by the latter ... But the Black Bonists are non-Buddhists; they are heretics. They take life, they kill animals for sacrificial purposes.

SIR CHARLES BELL

2
~

The Chinese Invasion
and After

On September 9 [1950], 3,000 troops of the 18th Route Army marched into Lhasa,

tubas and drums blaring, portraits of Mao and Zhou Enlai held aloft, between phalanxes of China's

red flag, one of whose four small orbits, circling the great yellow star at its center, was now Tibet.

JOHN AVEDON

*Main picture:
Crowds walk by
oblivious to a
giant poster of
Chairman Mao*

*Right: An
insubstantial and
ill-equipped Tibetan
army preparing
for the Chinese
invasion*

After several years of inner turmoil, China was finally united as a result of the creation of the People's Republic of China in 1949 under the new communist government headed by Mao Tsetung. Within the space of a few months the Chinese government announced publicly on Radio Peking their plans to "liberate" neighboring Tibet, along with Taiwan.

Tibet was at that time governed by a regency, the 14th Dalai Lama not yet having attained the necessary age to take up the reins of government. The original regent, Reting Rinpoche, had been removed from this powerful position following scandals concerning sexual misbehavior and general corruption. The new incumbent, Taktra Rinpoche, had also allowed corruption to flourish, though of a less serious nature, prompting a coup to regain power by the followers of Reting Rinpoche. This went awry and resulted in several days of fighting and bloodshed, which happened to coincide with China's new-found ascendancy.

Tibet was thus ill-prepared to deal with the threat of invasion. Generally a peaceloving country lacking the inclination to fight, Tibet had an army that was

In general, we Tibetans are very religious minded and there are many who are good practitioners as well, but believing the country would be saved without human effort, through prayers alone, resulted from limited knowledge.

14TH DALAI LAMA

Right: A man fatally wounded by Chinese police during a peaceful demonstration for Tibetan independence

insubstantial, badly equipped, and no match for the People's Liberation Army (PLA), which was well trained, fresh from victory, and enthusiastic to incorporate Tibet into "the Motherland." The Tibetan policy of "peaceful isolation" also reaped the consequence of the

Right: Jigme Taring, a Tibetan aristocrat from Lhasa, seen here as a soldier

country's pleas being dismissed by the United Nations when it appealed for help.

The People's Liberation Army initially made a minor excursion into eastern Tibet and took the town of Dengkok. The Chinese invaders were wiped out within a few weeks by a division of Khampas, traditionally the warriors of Tibet, renowned for their independence and willingness to avenge wrong deeds. However, this minor victory proved the only one, and a much larger division of the PLA regained Dengkok and the whole of Chamdo after an assault that began on October 7, 1950. The governor of the area, Ngabo, despite having the better military position, decided to flee and surrendered eleven days later.

> *Receiving word that the Chinese were only a day away in the east, while to the rear Riwoche was being surrounded, Ngabo lost his nerve. He radioed Lhasa for permission to surrender. When it was denied, he packed his belongings, took off the long gold and turquoise pendant earring hanging from his left ear, changed his yellow silk robes for the plain gray serge of a junior official and decamped in the middle of the night.*
>
> JOHN AVEDON

The Chinese announced their presence in Tibet on Radio Peking on October 25, stating that their troops were there to "free Tibetans from imperialist oppression." India immediately protested to China, but was sharply reprimanded for meddling in Chinese "internal affairs," leaving Nehru, the Indian leader, little chance to protest further without actively antagonizing his powerful neighbor. The progress of the Chinese occupation continued inexorably, culminating in a march to Lhasa in September, 1951.

Back in Lhasa, news of the loss of Chamdo filtered through and everyone began to realize the gravity of the situation. The government debated the issue intensely, while the people erected posters calling for the Dalai Lama to be given the power. Eventually the Gadong Oracle was called upon. The oracles, of which there were several, held a fascinating significance in Tibetan government: when serious issues arose, an oracle would be consulted. The oracle would speak through someone who would enter a trance and, then under the influence of the guardian spirits or deities

of Tibet, would make pronouncements about how the government should proceed. Over the years this had proved an effective aid to the more traditional methods of governing the country.

Now the oracle was called upon, and the medium went into a trance. When the guardian spirits entered his body, his strength increased considerably, and his attendants quickly strapped on the ceremonial head-dress. Normally the headdress was too heavy to be worn without support, but during the trance the oracle danced around as if it weighed almost nothing.

Left: The Chinese cavalry carrying their flags into Tibet

After offering the young Dalai Lama the traditional white scarf, known as a kata, the oracle was duly asked for advice by the ministers. "Make him king" was the reply just before the oracle collapsed, and the trance was ended.

Full of trepidation, the fifteen-year-old Tenzin Gyatso hesitated, reluctant to become both spiritual and temporal leader of his people so soon. However, he quickly realized this was not a personal choice, but a set of circumstances that he must make the best of, since the people of Tibet now needed the authority of the Dalai Lama.

Far right: The remains of Tse-Choling Monastery on the banks of the Kyichu River

Right: The Dalai Lama with Prime Minister Zhou Enlai, India, 1956

> *I could not refuse my responsibilities, I had to shoulder them, put my boyhood behind me and immediately prepare myself to lead my country.*
> 14TH DALAI LAMA

Thus, on November 17, 1950, according to the traditional ceremony held in the Potala, the 14th Dalai Lama was invested with the leadership of Tibet.

THE CHINESE OCCUPATION

For the next nine years the Dalai Lama dealt with the situation as best he could, but it soon became evident that the Chinese promise to help the Tibetans into the modern age by building roads and bringing in electricity merely disguised their true purpose. This was to sinocize Tibet and to bring it under total Chinese control by eroding Tibetan culture, language, and religion. The Chinese also mined for minerals, paying no respect to the land and its wildlife, and instigated programs of mass deforestation, trucking the wood to China.

The Dalai Lama was invited to China to admire a showcase of happy people living under communism,

and he had several meetings with Mao, but, increasingly aware of being manipulated, he remained inwardly skeptical, though outwardly diplomatic. Despite all the Chinese promises, the situation continued to worsen, and Tibet experienced its first serious food shortage due to the huge influx of Chinese soldiers. Despite its repeated pleas for assistance, no country would support Tibet, although as various atrocities came to light, international human-rights organizations started to condemn Chinese activity in Tibet. The situation continued to deteriorate, culminating in the Dalai Lama fleeing into exile.

THE CULTURAL REVOLUTION

Immediately after it was discovered that the Dalai Lama had fled, aware that he could no longer serve his country if he were detained by the Chinese authorities, pandemonium broke out. Heartily sick of Chinese interference in their lives, and with their beloved leader having been forced into exile, the Tibetans attacked their oppressors, venting the rage that had built up since the invasion. However, by now the Chinese forces were more powerful and better

armed than the Tibetans, and, after bitter fighting which resulted in thousands of dead, the Chinese emerged triumphant. This signaled the end of the pretence of the Chinese presence benefiting the Tibetans, and the systematic destruction and looting of all aspects of Tibetan culture, religion, and natural assets began in earnest.

Some improvements, as promised by the Chinese, did occur, but these were almost exclusively for the benefit of the increasing number of Chinese living in Tibet. Openly racist discrimination was practiced, and the Tibetan people started to become an underclass in their own country. Poverty, which was previously unknown, arrived and there was an increasing abuse of basic human rights. Dissent in any form was brutally repressed, and huge new prisons were built to hold the many Tibetans who felt unable to accept what was happening to their homeland and rebelled. The happiness and prosperity that had been promised under Chinese communism were realized to be slogans of lies and deception.

Meanwhile, back in China, another power struggle was being resolved. Mao's extremist ideological reforms had offended the moderate views of the president, Liu Shaoqi, and despite the failure of his first unification strategy, "The Great Leap Forward," Mao still managed to seize power in 1966. This heralded perhaps one of the most tragic epochs in modern human history, the Cultural Revolution, which resulted in greater suffering and death than occurred during World War II. However, China had closed its doors to the outside world, and only recently has the full story been revealed in all its nightmarish horror.

Tibet, along with other "minority areas," suffered even more than mainland China. Its citizens were

Right: Ganden Monastery in 1991, still partially in ruins, although some buildings have now been rebuilt

deemed to be reactionaries against the total uniformity of the proletariat by having their own language, religion, dress, and other cultural habits. On August 25, 1967, the Cultural Revolution arrived in Tibet, led by Red Guards in the persons of young, fanatical thugs who had been given free license to destroy. This was the tone of their inaugural declaration:

We, a group of lawless revolutionary rebels, will wield the iron sweepers and swing the mighty cudgels to sweep the old world into a mess and bash people into complete confusion.

While Western youth listened to the peace and love ballads of The Beatles and enjoyed an unprecedented freedom of self-expression, Tibetan youth witnessed their thousand-year-old culture being smashed and burned. Old and precious religious scriptures – the work of centuries – were burned in a five-day bonfire; beautiful antique Buddhist statues, paintings, and frescoes were desecrated and destroyed; historic buildings were reduced to rubble.

Degradation, humiliation, and torture accompanied the material destruction. Monks and nuns were forced to trample on and destroy sacred Buddhist images. Those who refused were beaten and dragged through the streets, where onlookers were made to spit on them and beat them further. Monks and nuns were forced to copulate publicly and were then made to participate in the breaking up of their monasteries. Lay people were ridiculed for wearing their traditional clothes and had their long braids cut off randomly in the streets; they were also beaten and forced to join the general destruction.

The Chinese government in Tibet, "The Great Alliance," was also attacked as "counter-revolutionary,"

but it was in a position to respond. After a few weeks of undisciplined rampaging and carnage, the Red Guards seized control of the main Tibetan newspaper and also attempted to gain control of the army, even succeeding in precipitating the flight of the head of the Communist Party in Tibet, Zhang Gouhua. Then the fighting started in earnest, with the old and new regimes battling for supremacy for nearly three years.

Though this was essentially a battle between Chinese factions, Tibetans were the main victims. The

Left: Tibetan prisoners in a truck accompanied by Chinese soldiers

existing Chinese government had at least been organized and consistent, and those Tibetans who rebelled knew what punishment they would receive. There was order, albeit repressive, but the Cultural Revolution spawned undisciplined and unpredictable violence.

Gangs of Red Guards roamed the streets, smashing anything Tibetan. Gang rape occurred, as well as random beatings and torture; even crucifixions were carried out alongside the spontaneous "thamzing" (public struggle) sessions, during which the participants had to confess to "crimes," and then their families were forced to beat them. The streets were unsafe, and houses were raided – frequently at night – and their occupants dragged away to prison, often without trial, for "counter-revolutionary activities." These included saying prayers (as religion was by now outlawed), or simply being a member of the educated or religious classes, including doctors.

Rapes and beatings turned into executions in which victims were forced to dig their own graves before being shot.

JOHN AVEDON

Once in prison, people were tortured to extract confessions. If they survived this stage, then re-education classes and forced labor followed, with such poor conditions that many died. So many Tibetans were imprisoned that surplus numbers were shipped elsewhere. They were sent to the Tengger Desert, a remote area near the border with Mongolia, where there was a huge complex of prison camps. Capable of housing almost ten million people, they had been built by the Chinese in the 1940s. Of the thousands of Tibetans sent there, only a few hundred returned, the usual prison death rate having been exacerbated by a two-year famine.

By 1970 stability had been regained, and the revolutionaries and the Great Alliance had formed the new Revolutionary Committee. The imprisonment and torture continued, however, and those who were not imprisoned were forced into the by now detailed destruction of their own culture, particularly the monasteries and religious artifacts. Anything of value that had survived destruction was shipped off to China. Otherwise, religious texts were used as wrapping paper or toilet tissue, the wooden blocks containing them were recycled as building materials; metal images and gilding were melted down; clay figures were thrown in the streets. Personal tragedy and cultural annihilation stood side by side.

Communes were formed both to maximize food production and to control groups of people. Everything now belonged to the state. There was no freedom of movement: people were assigned to a commune and had to remain there. Working in the fields filled the day; the evenings were used for propaganda sessions, in which Tibetans had to sing songs in praise of their "liberators" and renounce the Dalai Lama, their religion, and the old way of life. Failure to comply was punished by "thamzing." As the Chinese preferred to eat wheat, they tried to replace barley as the staple crop, a program that failed, and thus caused more famine. Consignments of unsuitable fertilizers were trucked in from China, which resulted in further ecological damage. Meanwhile, failures to produce target figures of grain were punished.

By 1975 the early disasters of commune farming were over, and sufficient barley was being grown. Chinese immigrants from the overpopulated mainland started to arrive in Tibet by the thousand. Large new towns, built in the Chinese style from concrete, sprang up, and the old, partly destroyed towns were repaired and expanded in this modern style. Along with its wildlife, much of its forests, and its traditional and religious way of life, the architecture of Tibet disappeared too. In 1976 earlier rumors were confirmed by American satellite that the Chinese nuclear facility at Lop Nor had been moved to Nagchuka, situated 165 miles (265 kilometers) north of Lhasa; thus Tibet entered the nuclear age as well.

MODERN TIBET

I cannot forget the present situation in Tibet, where neither discontent nor repression are confined to Lhasa.

14TH DALAI LAMA

Today Tibet remains an occupied country; its people a minority; its traditional culture and religion largely destroyed. However, things have improved, particularly following the death of Mao. There has been a relaxation of martial law, and the Tibetan religion may now be practiced, though it is not encouraged. Some of the excesses of the Cultural Revolution are being redressed, and almost a third of the monasteries have been partially or fully rebuilt. To the casual tourist, life in Tibet looks fine.

Oppression is now carried out through bureaucracy and is much more subtle. Patriotism is a

Above: Tibetan men, women, and children rebuilding Samye Monastery, 1986

prerequisite for religious practice: monks are now required to sign documents stating that they support the current regime, to undergo three months of "re-education," and to take an exam to prove that they have learned the material. It appears that the monasteries are not being interfered with, but the law is vague about how much religious practice is permitted.

Right: A Khampa man wearing a traditional hat with modern sunglasses, eastern Tibet, 1991

Only "normal" religious practice is tolerated, and this is not defined, leaving its interpretation conveniently open. To run a monastery you must be a known patriot, and some leading religious people are government spies. Lay officials now run two of the largest monasteries: Drepung and Sera. The numbers of monks per monastery are restricted and controlled.

There are roads, electricity, an airport, hotels for tourists, fax machines, karaoke bars, and discos. There are schools and hospitals, beggars and prostitutes. However, visitors trying to dip below this superficial normality can cause problems, and it is not a good idea to question Tibetans on politics because they are forbidden to criticize the party line. Policing is low profile these days: there have been no machine-gun posts on street corners since 1991, or tanks parading the roads since 1990, but some surveillance cameras are in evidence as well as a great number of plain-clothes policemen. Barracks full of riot police still exist, but they are tucked out of sight, and there remains a strong military presence in rural areas.

There are poster campaigns against the "splittists" – supporters of a free Tibet – but since they are in Chinese, most visitors miss their significance. These attack the Dalai Lama personally, saying that he is not a religious leader anymore and is furthermore a polit-ical traitor. But the average Tibetan who tows the line can travel outside Tibet now, though this takes time and needs connections, and travel within the country is also easier. Tibet has joined the modern world, though not in a way it would have chosen.

The world, meanwhile, remaining enthralled by Chinese trade opportunities, refuses politically to accept Tibetan independence and does not recognize the Tibetan government in exile. There has been some international activity concerning the Chinese abuse of human rights, however, and Tibet support groups now exist in many countries. China's record of human-rights abuse is well documented, though unfortunately this has not yet translated into political action, which remains unlikely unless a concerted international effort is made.

Left: Tibetan children playing in Lhasa

3
~

A Community
in Exile

When the horse runs on wheels and the iron bird flies,

the Tibetan people will be scattered like ants across the face of the earth.

PADMASAMBHAVA

After the Dalai Lama escaped to India, there were outbreaks of rioting throughout Lhasa, which were brutally put down by the Chinese. As the dominant force, they eventually subdued the Tibetans but not before thousands had died. This was the most severe incidence of large-scale violence so far during the occupation, and an indication of the oppression that was to follow. It prompted the first wave of people to leave their homes, families, friends, and the majority of their possessions and follow their leader into an unknown future in exile.

The Dalai Lama, meanwhile, had arrived in India on March 31, 1959, and been escorted to Mussoorie, where he lived during his first year in exile. Here news of hundreds of Tibetans crossing into India, Nepal, and Bhutan began to arrive, along with horrific tales of the battle in Lhasa. The Indian government was unprepared for such large numbers of refugees but hurriedly constructed transit camps in Missamari and Buxa Duar to accommodate them, while it worked out what to do.

Nehru had till now advocated trying to find a solution with the Chinese and refused to intervene, despite his fellow politicians' criticism of his handling of the situation, as it became evident that the Chinese invasion of Tibet was in the process of destroying this ancient nation. He was in a difficult political situation

Main picture: A Tibetan refugee inscribing sacred symbols on a rock in Manali, northern India

Left: Some of the first Tibetan refugees, newly arrived in India, 1959

and was loath to antagonize such a powerful neighbor, but his humanitarian principles endured, and he did his best to help those who arrived in India.

Many never survived the flight into exile. Chinese soldiers often shot those whom they caught attempting to leave. The perilous trek through high mountain passes, walking through deep snow and blizzards, claimed more lives, especially those of children and old people. Many arrived in India too weak and ill to survive for more than a few days or weeks, their physical condition aggravated by despair and grief. The refugees included orphans, mothers who had lost one or more children, and men – key figures in the assault on the Chinese who, fearing reprisals, had fled the country, leaving their families behind.

Above: An Indian official greets the Dalai Lama at an army post in Assam, 1959

The Tibetans are a hardy race, but their previous existence on "the roof of the world" had left them untouched by most diseases and ill-equipped to deal with a lower-altitude climate. Thus many succumbed to tuberculosis, digestive problems brought on by an unfamiliar diet and aggravated by malnutrition, and illness caused by the humid heat of the fast-approaching Indian summer. Clothing was another basic problem: the heavy clothes required for the Tibetan climate and the mountain walk to freedom were unsuitable in India.

By June 1959 the refugees numbered more than twenty thousand, swelled daily by new arrivals. The Dalai Lama had a meeting with Nehru in Delhi in

order to decide how best to proceed, because the transit camps were overflowing with refugees, many of whom were dying, and all were suffering from the unfamiliar humid heat. The newly formed Tibetan government in exile (called the Kashag), though officially unrecognized by the Indian government, had discussed with Indian officials a plan to employ the refugees building roads in the north. These road camps were situated at a higher altitude, lessening the exiles' suffering, and the road-building work would allow them to earn a living at subsistence level.

ADAPTING TO LIFE IN INDIA

Children, women, and men were all working side by side in gangs; former nuns, farmers, monks, officials, all thrown together. They had to endure a full day's hard physical toil under a mighty sun, followed by nights crammed into tiny tents.

14TH DALAI LAMA

This new life was tough and fraught with dangers, and the hard physical work took its toll on the people who were physically and emotionally weakened. The work was hazardous, with the danger of rock falls and crumbling, unprotected cliff edges, and the use of dynamite. Mingling with the local Indians brought them into contact with unfamiliar diseases, and the fatalities continued. A new issue arose at this time too: the children had to be cared for and educated. As Nehru told the Dalai Lama, "in your children lies your future."

Main picture: Tibetan refugees building the Leh road in the Kulu Valley, northern India

Below: The Dalai Lama (center) meeting Pandit Nehru (left), 1956

Nehru personally took an interest in the setting up of separate schools for the refugee Tibetan children and assured the Dalai Lama that the Indian government would fund this program. As well as helping to preserve their culture, these schools were also important so that these children could become a part of the modern and international world; to this end English was taught and was also used to teach the other subjects. Though this meant more separation for already dislocated families, the importance of educating their children and thereby preserving their cultural heritage was apparent, and fifty children were sent away to a new life at the first school in Mussoorie.

By September 1959, the refugees numbered almost thirty thousand, and another pressing concern had arisen. Many of the refugees were monks and high lamas, the religious persecution in Tibet having affected them the most. They arrived with as many sacred texts as they could carry in an attempt to save their precious Buddhist scripts from annihilation. However, they too were indiscriminately set to work on road building and had equally succumbed to disease and death.

We were eager to save our religion, but after just a few years the number of monks dying increased to the point that the rest couldn't help wondering whether or not we'd ever escape from that place alive.
KHENTRUL RINPOCHE

Much of the propagation of Tibetan Buddhism relied on the special relationship between a spiritual teacher and his disciples – known as guru devotion – with the result that a great deal of teaching was oral; each time a lama died some Buddhist wisdom and knowledge died too. Thus the Dalai Lama suggested that the high lamas find other work; a difficult task since they were untrained in secular activities.

This threat to the very heart of Tibetan culture had to be addressed as soon as possible, and Nehru asked the various states of India whether they would donate some land to the Tibetans to allow them to build their own communities. The first offer was of 3,000 acres near Mysore in southern India. This gift, kind though it was, caused several problems. The area was even hotter than that of the transit camps, and also a long way from Dharamsala, where the Dalai Lama would take up residence. The land was also undeveloped and heavily forested, so the new settlers would face harsh conditions in order to make it habitable.

However, the Dalai Lama gratefully accepted the gift, since by now all hopes of an imminent return to a free Tibet had been dashed; with every new refugee came a story of further violent repression. The Chinese were clearly there to stay.

Main picture:
Hanging new prayer flags to celebrate Losar, the Tibetan New Year

Below: Early refugee camp in Delhi in 1959

Above left: A Tibetan man wearing traditional clothing, central Tibet 1933

Above right: Refugees at a camp in Manali, northern India, 1970

Right: Corn growing in Manipat, India

Main picture:
A young Tibetan
girl with baby
sibling, Kulu valley,
northern India,
1970

Above left: Old
Tibetan woman
outside her house
in refugee camp,
southern India,
1995

Above right:
Tibetan refugee in
Manali, northern
India, 1970

Left: Tibetan
children in the
Kulu valley, 1970

The Dalai Lama's attempts to gain support from other countries, which were permitted but discouraged by Nehru, had met with little other than goodwill; no country of note would take up the issue of the Chinese occupation, though international condemnation of their human-rights abuse had started. Thus the Dalai Lama realized that his main task was to preserve and consolidate Tibetan religion and culture in exile.

A SUCCESS STORY

Many of the first six hundred and sixty-six settlers at Bylakuppe, southern India, burst into tears on their arrival in December 1960. Supplied with tents and a

Right: Monks eating rice during a break in teachings, Dharamsala

few basic tools, they were then left to clear the jungle and to try to make farmland and build villages. The enormity of the task was finally matched by the indomitable Tibetan spirit and by the encouragement of the Dalai Lama, but for the first couple of years, life was grim, with the air heavy with smoke from fires, making the heat almost unbearable. Wild animals proved dangerous too, particularly elephants, which rampaged periodically through the settlements.

Five hundred new settlers were sent down to Bylakuppe at six-month intervals; there were many fatalities, but the numbers of settlers slowly grew. By 1962 the first permanent residences were completed; a decade or so later there were twenty villages and six monasteries, housing ten thousand people. There were early farming failures, reflecting the very different land and climate that the Tibetans had to accommodate. But by adapting themselves, and with the aid of foreign agencies, they learned how to grow corn and ragi (a cereal crop) rather than their traditional barley. Dairy farms and fruit trees did well, but other attempts at animal husbandry failed, for the Tibetans' Buddhist beliefs in the sacredness of all life remained strong.

> *On my first visit to Bylakuppe I well remember the settlers being very concerned that the burning they were having to carry out to clear the land was causing the death of innumerable small creatures and insects. For Buddhists this was a terrible thing to be doing, since we believe that all life, not just human life, is sacred.*
>
> 14TH DALAI LAMA

Other settlements in Kalimpong, Orissa, and Arunachal Pradesh were established and developed over the years. Again various cooperatives were set up

with foreign aid, principally concentrating on carpet weaving, a skill the refugees brought from Tibet. But they also fitted into the local Indian community by developing tractor workshops and similar endeavors. A testament to their determination to survive can be seen in the fact that Bylakuppe was self-supporting in six years and making a profit in ten.

A NEW COMMUNITY

On April 30, 1960, the Dalai Lama and his entourage arrived at their new home in Dharamsala, or more accurately the little village lying a mile or so above it called McLeod Ganj. This used to be one of the places where the British took their summer vacations, far above the heat of the plains. It is set on the side of one of the foothills of the Himalayas, and on a clear day beautiful views can be enjoyed down to the valleys below and up to snow-clad mountain ranges.

> *It was quite late when we arrived so I was not able to see much, but the following morning, when I woke, the first thing I heard was the distinctive call of a bird which I later discovered is peculiar to this place… I looked out of the window to see where it was, but could not find it. Instead my eyes were greeted by a view of magnificent mountains.*
>
> 14TH DALAI LAMA

Such a comforting, familiar sight was a positive welcome to the place in which he still resides today.

Over the years McLeod Ganj has become a "little Tibet," with more than five thousand Tibetan refugees living in the immediate area. The Tibetan government in exile has a complex of buildings housing the offices of all its various departments, just around the corner

from the Library of Tibetan Works and Archives. As well as containing thousands of sacred texts and its own small publishing initiative, it houses a few priceless treasures that were rescued and smuggled over the mountains to safety. Classes in Tibetan Buddhism are also given to the increasing number of Westerners that arrive each year.

There are also several monasteries and nunneries in McLeod Ganj, as well as the Medical and Astrological Institute, where you can see a Tibetan doctor or buy traditional Tibetan medicine. The two main streets are lined with little shops, often with workshops at the back, selling carpets, bags, jewelry, and other Tibetan and Buddhist paraphernalia. There is a wide range of hotels and restaurants catering to all types of travelers and tourists. The Tibetan Institute of Performing Arts

Above: The Dalai Lama teaching at his monastery in Dharamsala

(TIPA) produces traditional folk dances, music, and songs. A few miles down the hillside lies the Norbulingka, where young Tibetans learn such traditional arts as thangka painting, the traditional Buddhist cloth paintings framed in silk brocade.

If you look behind the apparent prosperity, however, there are other stories to be discovered. Young monks, nuns, and children frequently approach tourists for sponsorship. The farther back from the main streets they are, the poorer the houses become, and the Tibetan Children's Village – a great success story of the early days – still does not have enough places for all Tibetan children. Some of the young Tibetans have become disillusioned about ever returning to a land that they have never known. Everywhere there are signs calling for a free Tibet, but many people accept they are in India to stay. In total, there are now over one hundred thousand Tibetan refugees living outside Tibet.

The life of a refugee is understandably difficult for the generation that fled from their homeland, but there is now a whole new generation of young Tibetans who have never seen their country, and who have different problems to overcome. Unemployment in the case of college graduates is severe; these people are not satisfied with selling Tibetan artifacts, and there are only limited opportunities available in the professions. Some young Tibetans have done quite well from sponsorship, but nevertheless feel a mixture of gratitude and resentment.

Young men wearing ponytails riding on motorcycles with their girlfriends is a phenomenon of youth culture with which we have all become familiar in the West. But here the boys are Tibetan and the girls tend to be Western. Recreational drug habits are beginning

to creep into their culture, too. Just as during the 1960s, when angry young people from Europe and America were rebelling against a restrictive culture, today's Tibetan youths also feel limited and alienated, because they have been forced to live in a country that is not their own. The often overly romantic Western perception of the Tibetan people is a projection that they do not want to live up to either.

Above: Turning prayer wheels in McLeod Ganj

Left: The Nechung Oracle at the Monlam festival, Drepung Monastery

TSERING'S STORY

Yet there is also a quiet optimism among Tibetan youth. Tsering is twenty-six, was born in Amdo, and escaped Tibet in 1992, though his first attempt to flee was unsuccessful. On that occasion he obtained the papers permitting him to travel to Lhasa and then headed for the border, walking and hitching rides. He was caught by Chinese guards near a famous stupa (a Buddhist shrine), and, aware of the reprisals of being caught trying to escape, fabricated a story:

I told them I was not educated, not a monk, only a simple farmer. This stupa has a reputation; if you see and circumambulate around it you will get a good rebirth and have no problems in this life. So I pretended I was very simple and had only wanted to do this. I was lucky: they believed me, so they took all my money, put me in prison for three days and then took me back to Lhasa.

Undeterred, Tsering tried again; this time with a friend who had money and a permit that would get them near the border. They walked for seven days to an isolated place from which they could cross the border into Nepal, but then met some robbers:

They were good robbers, they didn't want to kill us. My friend had put a little money in his shoe – we knew we might meet robbers here – but they took all the rest of his money and jewelry. I had no money for them to steal, since the guards had taken all mine before. We just carried on walking. Then we started to see trees we had never seen before, so we knew we had made it into Nepal. I felt very happy.

Tsering spent a few months in Nepal and then came to McLeod Ganj. When he discovered that the school for new refugees had no classroom and that lessons were held sitting on the grass, he felt that he could do better by himself and managed to get a good job working for a German aid agency in a local office. (In 1992 it was easier for an educated young Tibetan to get a job.)

Now I have a room and a job and I'm happy. I can do and say what I like. In Tibet a Chinese official told me I did not even have the right to listen to the radio; this was when I decided to leave. I miss my family but I can write to them and they are happy I have come here and made a new life. I would like to improve my English and eventually do research and translation. I don't want a sponsor; I have seen it makes people greedy. One day two sponsors [of a friend of mine] who did not know about each other, turned up together. Very embarrassing! I think because religion is the soul of the Tibetan people that perhaps it is not possible to separate religion and politics. In another ten to twenty years I think the Chinese will have destroyed the majority of Tibetan culture and religion in Tibet.

Yet while Tsering told me his tale over a cup of tea he was smiling and laughing, not bitter or resentful. He accepts what has happened, that this is how it is, and is getting on with his life. When we walked down the street he knew almost everyone – Tibetan and Western – and often stopped to talk. He is refreshingly open and charming, but modest. When I told him that I was writing a book and asked if I could use his story, he replied that of course I might, but he wasn't sure if he was very interesting – I could find many other, better stories. It may come to pass that the Chinese will eventually destroy the old way of life in Tibet, but the spirit of the Tibetans will live on in people like Tsering.

THE CURRENT SCENE

Other countries also have small Tibetan communities, notably Switzerland, which provided foster families for Tibetan orphans in the 1960s and is home to perhaps the most prosperous Tibetan community in exile. There was a lottery program that provided a thousand places for Tibetans in the United States, which has proved successful, though there were some early problems, and Tibetans experienced alienation in adapting to such a different society. Further groups have since joined the original refugees, and close family members have now been permitted to join the first group. The increasing popularity of Tibetan Buddhism has also created a number of Tibetan Buddhist centers in many countries around the world, with at least one resident lama in each center.

The early settlements in southern India have survived and flourished, and the three greatest monasteries of Tibet have been painstakingly recreated: Ganden and Drepung at Mundgod, and Sera at Bylakuppe. Thousands of young monks are studying with the few surviving great teachers to have lived in Tibet, and there seems to be no shortage of young monks, despite the allure of Indian or Western ways of life. The monasteries are surrounded by villages where farmers, carpet weavers, traders, and schoolchildren live and work.

Though these settlements are situated off the tourist trail and require special permits in order to visit them, it is possible to do so. Participating in one of the several hour-long Buddhist ceremonies, which start before dawn, gives you a glimpse of life in these monasteries. You sit in a sea of maroon-robed monks, listening to the sonorous chanting of ancient Tibetan prayers, surrounded by huge, gilded statues of the Buddha and bodhisattvas (similar to Christian saints). Young monks run in with large kettles of Tibetan tea and baskets of unleavened Tibetan bread, which is cheerfully consumed during the ceremony. The ritual seems timeless, and the spirit of Tibet is thereby kept alive, albeit in foreign lands.

Far left: A crowd of Tibetans at Dharamsala, watching a street performance

Left: Tibetan monks sitting on a motorcycle, Dharamsala, 1997

Below: Monks playing frisbee near Rumtek, Sikkim

One of the major concerns for the Dalai Lama is the Chinese occupation of Tibet. The following extracts are from the many speeches, press conferences, interviews, and public talks where he addresses the situation.

TO THE TIBETAN PEOPLE

In general what you experience during hard times is the best lesson. Therefore we have learned a lot over the past years since [the] Chinese occupation. During this period the Chinese have created such enormous problems, but the main advice in Mahayana Buddhism is that there is no point in taking revenge. The Tibetans who can understand this advice will not have any bad feelings towards the Chinese. I used to say China has eaten Tibet, but cannot digest it; now that still seems to be true.

TIBET ON THE WORLD STAGE

Firstly we need a sense of global responsibility. Time is always changing, and particularly in the field of economy much has changed. Today's reality is heavily interdependent – that is its nature – and there are strong links between human behavior and ecology. Each country is dependent on its neighbor, and the concept of "we" and "they" is already, I think, out of date.

The spirit of nonviolence is very much relevant in today's world to resolve conflict, and I consider nonviolent action is the manifestation and expression of compassion. We should not consider this a sign of weakness but of strength. So long as human intelligence exists there will always be contradiction, and logically the best way to solve this is [through] nonviolent action, dialog.

Tibet needs more development, and Tibet cannot do this effectively alone. Therefore, if we join partly with another big nation we may get greater benefit. So as soon as some positive indication comes from the Chinese government I am ready to talk and negotiate without any preconditions. So I appeal to you, please help us.

I really appreciate the media [they are] very supportive … you analyze the facts from various sources, and then you come to the conclusion that things are not happy as the Chinese government states. You investigate reality, and I consider that pro-justice, rather than pro-Tibetan.

I believe it is only a question of time before the Tibetan situation is resolved; things will change. Meanwhile I will remain a little bit stubborn! Also in recent times some Chinese artists, writers, intellectuals, and students are seeing the reality and are critical of Chinese government policy. There is better awareness now of the failures of the Chinese government policies. Some people have sincere concern, like the Chinese involved in the democratic movement, and are showing us solidarity; this I think is very encouraging.

PRESS CONFERENCE, LONDON, JULY 1996

FREE TIBET!

PROTECTING TIBETAN CULTURE, ECONOMY, AND ENVIRONMENT

My main aim is the preservation of Tibetan culture. If Tibet remains divided into separate regions and their cultural heritage is assimilated into Chinese culture, then there is no hope. Tibetan-Buddhist culture has great potential to create a peaceful human community, not only in Tibet. Buddhist culture is already helping revive the old Russian republics of Buryat, Kalmyck, and Tuva. The local people were historically Buddhist, with the same Tibetan-Buddhist tradition, but their culture was nearly lost.

The most important people Tibetan Buddhism can benefit are the Chinese. Amdo Lama, who lives in Beijing, has been giving Buddhist courses to small Chinese audiences for ten to fifteen years. Recently a Chinese journalist brought me a picture of a Chinese high military commander in full uniform, just sitting very seriously in meditation. So we can see that when China becomes more open, with more freedom, then definitely many Chinese will find useful inspiration from Tibetan-Buddhist tradition.

Some environmentalists believe that the natural balance and climate in the Tibetan plateau is very important for normal monsoon in the lands surrounding the Himalayas. Indiscriminate mining without precautions and massive deforestation brings a lot of erosion. There is also the problem of dumping nuclear waste. There is a danger of contaminating all the major rivers in that part of the world; the Ganges, Brahmaputra, Yellow, Yangtze, and Mekong rivers, all these have their ultimate source in Tibet.

So if something happens on the roof of the world, then a vast area in east, southeast, and south Asia is affected. According to ecologists, the high altitude and dry climate is more delicate, and once damage happens it takes a longer period to recover. The Tibetan environment is a very, very serious matter. So this also, for some people, is a matter of real concern.

We need genuine self-rule. It is essential for the Tibetans to have the full responsibility, taking care of the environment, conserving the resources, and looking out for the interests of Tibetan workers, nomads, and farmers. The Chinese have shown a consistent concern to get profits as quickly as possible, regardless of the effect on the environment. Unfortunately they simply have the intention to make money quickly, with no consideration of whether that industry benefits the local Tibetans or not.

Therefore, it is important that responsibility for the development of Tibet must be carried out by the Tibetans themselves. There must be genuine self-rule, for the protection of Tibetan culture, economy, and environment. In other fields, such as foreign affairs and defense, perhaps we cannot carry all the responsibility. Buddhism became so central for Tibetans that, for the last two centuries, we have had some kind of general demilitarization. So practically it is easier for us to let the Chinese government assume these responsibilities.

INTERVIEW WITH ROBERT THURMAN

Above: Protest outside the Chinese embassy, London

Top left: A Chinese soldier installs the Chinese flag, Tibet, 1986

Center: "Visualize peace in Tibet," Dharamsala, 1997

Left: Monks pray during a protest commemorating the Tibetan uprising

4
~

The Dalai Lama,
Leader of the Tibetans

From the beginning I was groomed for the day when, in addition to my position

as spiritual leader of Tibet, I would assume temporal leadership as well.

14TH DALAI LAMA

Main picture:
The Dalai Lama
at a conference of
lamas in Varanasi,
northern India

Right: The Dalai
Lama constructing
a Kalachakra
sand mandala,
Bodhgaya,
northern India

The idea of a king or queen ruling a country seems somewhat dated to Europeans, and has not been experienced by Americans. Yet this is the role of the Dalai Lama, a priest-king who is both a spiritual and temporal leader of his country. The current 14th Dalai Lama, who is aware of the potential dangers and lack of democracy that this position could entail, has sought to reduce his political influence, but it is extremely interesting that this policy has met with much resistance from many of the Tibetan people. The reasons for their reaction are more to do with the history and tradition of Tibet, rather than arising from any disrespect of democracy.

Before the institution of the Dalai Lamas, Tibet swung between periods of stability, under either a benign or an exploitative ruler, and times of unrest and fighting when a rival faction sought power, or when Tibet's Mongolian or Chinese neighbors invaded the country and took over. Tibet comprises three main regions and has four main sects of Buddhism, so various alliances between lamas and powerful laymen arose as a matter of course. These factions either succeeded in taking power unaided, or with assistance from a neighboring ruler.

In the late fourteenth century, a brilliant monk named Tsongkhapa attracted many disciples, and a new Buddhist order accordingly developed. Emphasizing the ethical values of Buddhism and the doctrinal purity of the eleventh-century Indian teacher Atisha, the new sect became known as the Geluk ("Virtuous Order") and acted as a counterpoint to the other Buddhist traditions, most of which had strayed into the worldly and corrupt arena of politics. This renaissance of Buddhist ideology proved to be enduring, and leadership of the Gelukpas was then passed to Tsongkhapa's nephew, Gendun Drup. He declared that after his death he would be reborn as a Tibetan and left clues as to how his followers could find his successor.

Next in line was Gendun Gyatso, followed by Sonam Gyatso, who both served the tradition well, and it continued to expand. The Mongolians — who were always interested in their neighbor's power games — noted the ascendancy of the Gelukpas, and their leader, Altan Khan, invited Sonam Gyatso to meet him. The Mongolian leader was impressed by the purity of this Buddhist teacher, gave him the title of Dalai Lama, and encouraged his own people to convert to Buddhism.

Dalai is Mongolian for "ocean," *Lama* is Tibetan for "spiritual teacher," hence the common, if slightly embellished, translation "Ocean of Wisdom." The Dalai Lamas are also considered to be manifestations of Chenrezig, the Buddha of compassion, and therefore to embody in human form the spiritual ideal of compassion. The title of Dalai Lama was retrospectively conferred upon Sonam Gyatso's two predecessors, and thus the tradition that has endured to this day was established.

The succession of Dalai Lamas is continued through reincarnation, as is the succession of other highly realized teachers, called tulkus. When the Dalai Lama dies, his followers look for omens and consult oracles for clues as to where to look for the child who will become the next Dalai Lama. This system has the drawback of needing a regent to fill in while the child grows up. The rule of the regents has proved disastrous for most of the Dalai Lamas – many of whom never survived to take power themselves – except the 5th, the 13th, and the current 14th Dalai Lama.

A NEW FORM OF GOVERNMENT

The Dalai Lama and the Kashag, or cabinet, formed the heart of the Tibetan government in exile, and they were supplemented by various departments, offices, and an elected commission, a system that continues today with a few modifications. The Tibetan Youth Congress has now been formed and has come to function as a sort of "loyal opposition" party. Many of the young Tibetans, born in exile, hold modern and radical views that are useful counterpoints to those of the official cabinet. Formal communication between them has been strongly encouraged by the Dalai Lama. Between them, they carry out all the usual business of state and function in the same way as any other legislative body, although they remain officially unrecognized – as they were at their inception – by all but one or two small countries.

The Dalai Lama's enthusiasm for democracy led to the first elections in 1960, shortly after the Tibetans' arrival in Dharamsala and before their constitution was finalized. The ballots seemed strange to the Tibetans, who had no experience of how to vote.

Far left: The Dalai Lama riding an elephant in Bodhgaya

TABLE OF THE 14 DALAI LAMAS

~

1	Gendun Drup	1391 - 1474
2	Gendun Gyatso	1476 - 1542
3	Sonam Gyatso	1543 - 1588
4	Yonten Gyatso	1589 - 1616
5	Ngawang Losang Gyatso	1617 - 1682
6	Tsangyang Gyatso	1683 - 1706
7	Kelsang Gyatso	1708 - 1757
8	Jampel Gyatso	1758 - 1804
9	Lungtog Gyatso	1805 - 1815
10	Tsultrim Gyatso	1816 - 1837
11	Khedrup Gyatso	1838 - 1855
12	Trinle Gyatso	1856 - 1875
13	Tubten Gyatso	1876 - 1933
14	Tenzin Gyatso	1935 -

Far right: The Dalai Lama and Father Lawrence Freeman at a Buddhist/Christian conference, England 1995

Below: Talking with the former archbishop of Canterbury, Robert Runcie, in London, 1989

A lot of people go into the election tent and just pray to His Holiness. "I don't know any of these candidates, but please let me choose the right one to help the Dalai Lama and the people." Then they put their finger down and ask the election officer, "Would you see whose name is here?"

LODI GYARI, 1975

When the constitution was announced a year later, there was uproar over the clause that allowed for the Dalai Lama to be impeached by a two-thirds majority, should this be felt necessary. The Dalai Lama's

provision for a reduction of his, or his successor's, own powers was an aspect of democracy that most of the Tibetan people found hard to accept. Finally, the constitution was ratified including the contentious clause, but only after much persuasion by the Dalai Lama. Their faith and belief in their leader makes it unlikely that the Tibetans would ever dream of using this power, but its existence is important for an authentic democracy.

A CONTEMPORARY ROLE

The Dalai Lama is in demand internationally because of the interest in Tibetan Buddhism around the world. His contributions at conferences on science, ecology, and interfaith issues are warmly received.

The Dalai Lama continues to speak out about the plight of the Tibetan people and the Chinese occupation of Tibet at every opportunity. This is a difficult role for him to play these days. He returns to countries where he spoke a few years ago about the urgency to help the situation in Tibet, yet there has been little change. The same dedicated faces greet him and renew their pledges of support, but they are unable to coerce their governments into taking constructive action. Tibet support groups stage demonstrations, hold benefit concerts, and send out newsletters, but to little practical effect. Occasionally a campaign to release a Tibetan political prisoner is successful, but it is a drop in the ocean.

Perhaps the new British Labour government will make a stand against the Chinese, since it has pledged to focus on human rights when dealing with foreign governments. The recent reversion of Hong Kong from being a British territory to a Chinese one may have a wider impact, particularly since it came only a

few months into the Labour Party's long-awaited rise to power. But President Bill Clinton suggested that he might take a tougher stance with regard to the Chinese government and then renewed its "most favored nation" status without negotiating the issue of human rights. It is thus obvious that the Chinese occupation of Tibet is a delicate political issue that has no simple solutions.

Despite this, whenever the Dalai Lama speaks on the Tibetan situation, he displays a total commitment to his cause. He welcomes any dialog with the Chinese, though little is forthcoming. He is obviously saddened and tired by the situation, yet he speaks with passion and equanimity – even humor – and inspires people wherever he goes. During Buddhist teaching sessions, public talks, and conferences, he spontaneously speaks about the situation; it is never far from his mind. His popularity as an international figure facilitates his role as leader of the Tibetans.

I hope and pray that soon the truth will prevail and the historical rights of my people will be restored, and to this end I reaffirm my commitment to this struggle.

14TH DALAI LAMA

These days, the Dalai Lama is a busy man. As a result, he is often away from Dharamsala on a foreign visit, much to the disappointment of the many tourists who arrive knowing that this place is his home. When in residence, there is also much work to do; meeting with lamas, monks, and the other members of the government, giving interviews, and finding time for his own spiritual practice.

Yet, despite his busy schedule, there is one thing he never fails to do, which is to try personally to greet all

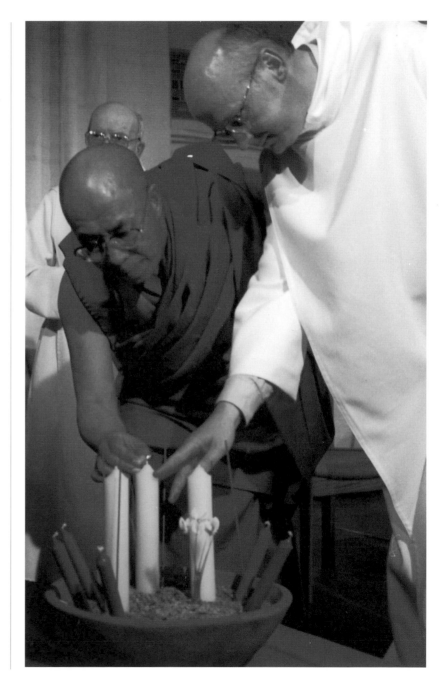

the Tibetans who arrive in Dharamsala. Not all are refugees; some are visiting family members and will return to Tibet because of some commitment or because they wish to be in their own country, despite living under Chinese rule. Many still come into exile however, often telling tales of repression and poverty.

It is a moving sight; long lines of people queuing patiently, often looking a little bewildered in this new place that they will shortly call "home." There is suddenly a commotion; the Dalai Lama has come out and has started to greet the first ones, holding their hands and giving them blessings. Sometimes he speaks with someone for a while, hearing some tale before moving on. The atmosphere is full of crying and joyous exclamations, as the exiles meet their genuinely beloved leader. This is no idle tourist attraction or public relations exercise, and non-Tibetan bystanders often move on, feeling rather voyeuristic, because it seems a strangely private event.

Below: The Dalai Lama receiving the Nobel Peace Prize, Stockholm, December, 1989

I try to greet all these visitors and new arrivals from Tibet in person. Invariably our meetings are very emotional; most are such sad innocent people, ragged and destitute. I always ask them about their own lives and families. And always there are tears when they reply – some breaking down entirely as they relate their pitiful stories.

14TH DALAI LAMA

The hope that they will one day return to a free Tibet is still alive in the dreams of the Tibetan exiles, but there are no longer the rumors of several years ago, and it is not talked about as much. Despite being officially refugees, their government unrecognized, their country not acknowledged as being independent, the Tibetans have nevertheless managed to survive extremely well in exile, some individuals having even become quite prosperous. Indeed, the exiles comprise the most successful refugee community, to the occasional chagrin of their Indian neighbors who are sometimes poorer. They are also managing to preserve much of their cultural and spiritual heritage in exile.

This survival is largely due to the skill of the Dalai Lama, his international status and high profile guaranteeing international aid and ensuring the condemnation of the human-rights abuses that continue in Tibet. Despite his democratization of the Tibetan government in exile, the majority of Tibetans still regard him as a "god-king," their faith in him remaining unshaken and their devotion as strong as ever. In the arena of world politics, the Dalai Lama's status is an almost unique phenomenon, and is a testament to a leader who combines spirituality with politics in an impressive way.

Left: The Dalai Lama conducting a ceremony in India, 1980

part two
~
a PORTRAIT
of the
DALAI LAMA

5
~

A Childhood in Tibet

When you look back to the time when Tibet was still a free country, I realize that those were the best years of my life.

14TH DALAI LAMA

On July 6, 1935, a boy was born to a family living in the village of Taktser, in Amdo, northeastern Tibet. His parents' fifth child, he was named Lhamo Thondup and was to all appearances a normal healthy baby. His family were one of about twenty in this remote settlement, making a living as farmers. Life was contented and unremarkable until Lhamo Thondup was nearly three years old.

One day, a group of traveling merchants arrived at the house and asked to make tea in the kitchen, a usual Tibetan custom. In reality, the group was a search party in disguise, looking for the new reincarnation of the Dalai Lama, and had been led to this area and the actual house by a series of signs and visions that had manifested since the death of the 13th Dalai Lama. Kewtsang Rinpoche, a high lama in charge of the expedition, was dressed as a servant and was therefore shown to a seat in the kitchen. There he was

approached by a small boy who climbed onto Kewtsang's knees with a familiarity that was unusual for such a young child.

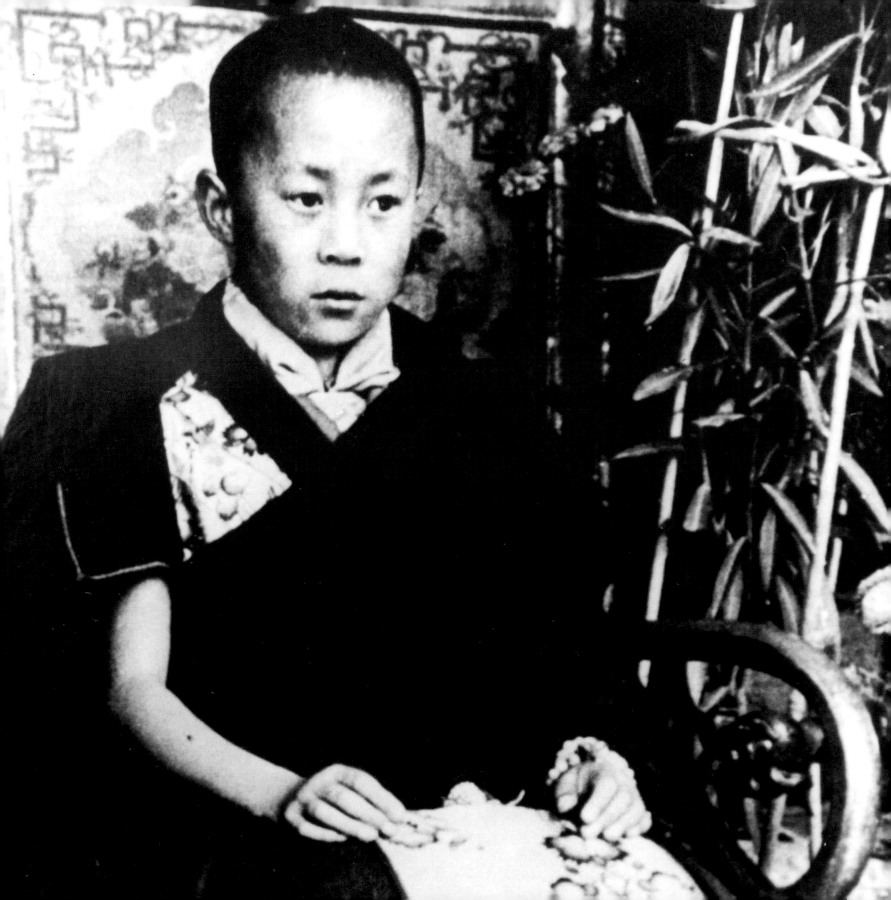

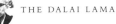

Taking hold of the prayer beads around the "servant's" neck, which had belonged to the 13th Dalai Lama, the boy demanded to be given them, saying that they were his. Kewtsang Rinpoche replied that he could have the prayer beads if Lhamo Thondup could tell him who he was. To his amazement, the little boy calmly told him that Kewtsang Rinpoche was a lama from Sera Monastery and did so in the dialect of central Tibet, which he could not have known. The party was invited to stay the night and, noticing further evidence of the child's extraordinary nature, the group's members decided to return with a proper delegation to conduct other tests to see if Lhamo Thondup was indeed the 14th Dalai Lama.

A few days later, they returned with other objects for the child formally to identify, which he did unerringly. He also underwent a brief physical examination to look for the eight traditional physical characteristics that distinguish Dalai Lamas, such as large ears and long eyes, with the eyebrows curving upward. Finding several of these attributes on the child as well, they realized that they were indeed in the presence of the 14th Dalai Lama. They were filled with joy and devotion.

Indeed we were so moved that tears of happiness filled our eyes. Scarcely able to breathe, we could neither sit properly on the mat nor speak a word.

SONAM WANGDU

Once news of the discovery became public, the local governor, a Muslim named Ma Bufeng, decided to profit from this exceptional event and refused to release the new Dalai Lama unless a ransom was paid. The quite large sum demanded took some time to raise, and after a few weeks, the young boy was sent

Left: The recently enthroned Dalai Lama, age five

Main picture: Monks gathered in a courtyard at Kumbum Monastery, Amdo

to Kumbum Monastery. It was usual to send children to be monks at a young age in order for them to adjust to the monastic way of life quickly; however, the first weeks were difficult, because the young boys inevitably missed their parents.

The Dalai Lama was no exception and recalls that this was an unhappy time for him for the most part. An older brother, Lobsang Samten, was already at the monastery and looked after him well, despite being only six himself. This was a great consolation. His

Left: The family of the 14th Dalai Lama at the Dekyi Lingka, 1946

brother's teacher, a kindly old monk, would also hold him wrapped in his robe whenever the young boy felt particularly lonely. However, he did not fully understand what it meant to be the Dalai Lama, and the months of waiting for the ransom money to be raised seemed interminable.

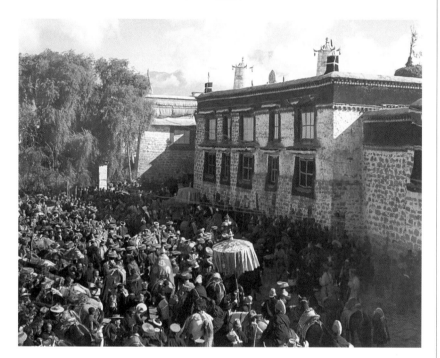

Above: The new Dalai Lama's arrival in Lhasa, October 10, 1939

About eighteen months later, when the ransom had been paid, but before the regent had given official confirmation that this was indeed the Dalai Lama in case Ma Bufeng caused further delays, the four-year-old Dalai Lama finally embarked upon his new life with the long journey to Lhasa. Happily reunited with his parents and thrilled at the prospect of traveling, the Dalai Lama recalls that the following three months were full of wonder as he saw the spectacular scenery unfolding each day. He remembers particularly the herds of wild asses, deer, and yaks that would suddenly appear, running across the vast plains. This memory is also tinged with sadness since these creatures are now mostly extinct. He also recalls squabbling with his brother frequently, as most young boys tend to do!

As it turned to fall, the party arrived outside the city gates and were welcomed into a ceremonial tent surrounded by huge crowds jostling each other to catch a glimpse of the new Dalai Lama. Inside the boy was seated on a wooden throne and in a day-long ceremony, officially became the spiritual leader of his people. His entourage then went to live at the Norbulingka, normally only the summer residence, the regent having decided to wait a year before enthroning the young boy at the Potala. So the less formal and more pleasant summer palace became the boy's home for his last year of carefree childhood.

THE EARLY YEARS IN LHASA

The following winter, when Lhamo Thondup was five, he was taken to the Potala and officially enthroned as spiritual leader of Tibet. From there, he went to the Jokhang temple to be ordained. His head was shaved after the regent performed the traditional hair-cutting ceremony, and he was dressed in the maroon robes of a monk. He was also given new names, traditionally including some of the regent's names, as well as that of Tenzin Gyatso, which is the name he goes by today.

Shortly afterward he started his education – which at the beginning consisted only of learning to read – together with his brother, Lobsang Samten. His brother was sent to school when Tenzin Gyatso was eight, and thereafter his companions were mostly adult men, sweepers, kitchen attendants, and the high lamas

Left: Pilgrim at the monument in Takster village where the present Dalai Lama was born

who were his senior and junior tutors. The first senior tutor, Reting Rinpoche, was removed from his position as a result of charges of corruption while the Dalai Lama was still quite young. Despite his youth and inexperience, Tenzin Gyatso was asked whom he thought the replacement should be. He suggested the junior tutor, Ling Rinpoche. This appointment was agreed upon, and Ling Rinpoche now became the senior tutor. Thus the Dalai Lama also learned about taking power and responsibility.

On a normal day, the young Dalai Lama would get up at around 6 a.m. and say prayers and meditate for an hour. Before the first study period, he would be brought a breakfast of tea, tsampa, and honey. Lessons, which progressed from reading to writing and the memorization of religious texts, finished at around 10 a.m., when he attended government meetings. These were formal affairs during which all due respect was paid to the Dalai Lama, although in the early years he was just a young child. In this way he learned both the business of government and the role that he would increasingly play as its leader.

Another study period followed, during which he would recite the text that he had learned earlier, and the junior tutor, Trijang Rinpoche, would introduce the text for the following day. His favorite activity – playing as is usual for a small child – occurred before lunch. Visiting foreign officials would bring him such toys as Meccano sets (kits of mechanical items, for

Above: Kyabje Trijang Rinpoche, junior tutor to the Dalai Lama, 1978

Right: A Tibetan teacher with his disciple

assembly into cars, cranes, etc.), clockwork-train sets, and lead soldiers. The young Dalai Lama thoroughly enjoyed playing war games with the latter, but when he became a teenager, he preferred to melt them down and recast them as monks. He also relished such physical games as sliding along the polished floors, as well as a jumping game that, although officially forbidden, was much indulged in.

After lunch were more lessons. The Dalai Lama recalls how the room in which he was taught lost the sun at about the same time as lessons started, resulting in a gloomy atmosphere that induced a certain reluctance to study. However, he was a bright pupil and learned quickly. The monastic curriculum included five major and five minor subjects, of which the most important was Buddhist philosophy, which was divided into further categories.

Dialectics, which is performed in a debating style, is fundamental to the Tibetan Buddhist system. It is quite spectacular to watch, or to engage in. Two monks take turns in asking each other questions on the finer philosophical meaning of a text. This is performed with the ritual gestures of slapping the right hand – with prayer beads wrapped around the wrist – into the left and simultaneously stamping the left foot while the question is asked.

Above: Ling Rinpoche, senior tutor to the 14th Dalai Lama

The responding partner attempts to sit passively and remain focused despite this activity, and then puts his own point across. By the time he reached the age of twelve, the Dalai Lama had started to practice debating in earnest, with two renowned experts.

His studies ended at around 5:30 p.m. and then there were a couple of free hours before dinner. He recalls rushing outside onto the roof of the Potala with his telescope and watching the inmates of the state prison far below.

I considered them to be my friends and kept a close eye on their movements. They knew this and whenever they caught sight of me threw themselves down in prostration. I recognized them all and always knew when someone was released or there was a new arrival.

14TH DALAI LAMA

Below: Lhamo Thondup, age three, by which time he had already been recognized as the 14th Dalai Lama

Dinner consisting of tea, soup, perhaps a little meat, yogurt, and bread was followed by a twilight walk while reciting scriptures and saying prayers, or making up stories, which, when younger, the Dalai Lama much preferred. Then he retired to his bedroom; this was the same room used by the 5th Dalai Lama and had hardly been touched since. Mice nested in the ancient bedding, feeding off the daily offerings of food placed on the altar, and the room was old and musty, cold and dimly lit. The Dalai Lama would snuggle into the cushion-filled wooden box that was swathed with red drapes that served as the bed, and fall asleep listening to the scampering of mice, the air filled with incense and the smell of burning butter lamps.

GROWING UP

There was not much deviation from this daily routine, except on festival days and during the periods of intense meditation and prayers called retreats. Nonetheless, there was still time for hobbies and exploring the labyrinth of rooms in the Potala in the winter. The Dalai Lama found an old projector, which he quickly learned how to use, having an aptitude for mechanical things. He also enjoyed taking watches apart and mending them again, after an initial disaster when he opened the back of a watch and the internal clockwork sprang out all over the floor!

At the Norbulingka, to his delight and excitement, he found three old automobiles that had been imported by his predecessor. Together with a mechanically minded assistant who had been the driver for the 13th Dalai Lama, he managed to combine their parts and eventually get one of the automobiles running. Unable to resist the temptation, one day he drove it around the parkland of the Norbulingka. However, not having learned to drive properly, he hit a tree and somewhat shamefacedly returned the automobile to the garage, managing to conceal the broken headlamp from his assistant with sticky tape and paint.

Occasionally the Dalai Lama's mother and older sister, Tsering Dolma, would visit, bringing him homebaked bread, which he loved. The family lived in a house in the grounds of the Norbulingka, and he would sometimes sneak over for a visit and there receive other treats, such as dried-meat strips dipped in chili sauce, though this was not officially allowed. The Dalai Lama remembers that the formal protocol surrounding him was sometimes oppressive and he encouraged informality as soon as he could; a manner that he retains today.

Left: Prayer flags
by a pile of rubble,
possibly a desecrated
holy building,
central Tibet

He also befriended an escaped Austrian prisoner of war who had found his way to Lhasa from a British prison camp in India. He learned about the outside world from his new companion, Heinrich Harrer, who wrote the book *Seven Years in Tibet* about his time in the country and his friendship with the young Dalai Lama. Harrer helped him with his English studies and also with fixing the various imported mechanical objects from the 13th Dalai Lama's time that had fallen into disrepair.

In 1947, when he was twelve, the Dalai Lama had his first experience of political intrigue when the deposed first regent, Reting Rinpoche, forcibly attempted to take back the regency, resulting in an armed fight during which many of his followers died. The Dalai Lama heard shots being fired and, after his initial excitement, sadly realized this sound meant that

people had died. Shortly afterward, Reting Rinpoche died mysteriously in prison. Increased security, particularly at his first public debating session at Drepung Monastery soon afterward, made sure the Dalai Lama did not forget this first lesson on the struggle for power and its often tragic consequences.

This was the world of the young Dalai Lama, which continued mostly peacefully until he was fifteen. October, 1950, brought the first wave of the Chinese invasion, however, and his age of innocence was swept away as eighty thousand soldiers marched into Chamdo and started the "peaceful liberation" of Tibet. From now until his escape in March, 1959, this child-monk had to mature into the leader of an occupied country and of a people who would suffer terribly at the hands of their oppressors.

6
~

A New Life
in India

*Today I am definitely happy, but inevitably the existence I now lead
is very different from the one I was brought up to.*

14TH DALAI LAMA

For almost a decade from 1950 to 1959 the Dalai Lama attempted to deal with the Chinese authorities who had assumed power after their successful invasion of Tibet in September, 1950. Aware that his cooperation would be useful in implementing their new policies, the Chinese government gave the Dalai Lama and his government a token role of sharing power. In reality, this was little more than a façade, but nonetheless he was able to help slow down the inevitable changes. As the traditional way of life was gradually dismantled, the situation steadily deterio-rated, particularly the religious practices that were so integral to the Tibetan existence. Such Chinese inter-ference was disrespectful and insensitive, obviously aimed at reducing the role that religion played in everyday life. The Dalai Lama consistently tried to win concessions for the Tibetan people, but he was regarded by the Chinese as an irritating tooth that would one day be pulled.

Left: The Dalai Lama with his younger brother during their escape from Tibet

Main picture: Refugees newly arrived from Tibet at the Kathmandu reception center, 1997

By the spring of 1959, the Tibetans felt that they had put up with enough from their unwanted new rulers and were merely waiting for an incident as an excuse to let loose their pent-up wrath. It was not long in coming. Shortly after the Dalai Lama had been awarded his Geshe degree in Buddhist studies (roughly equivalent to a Ph.D.), General Chiang Chin-wu, taking advantage of the traditional New Year greetings, invited the Dalai Lama to see a Chinese dance troupe that was newly arrived in Lhasa. The suggested venue was the Chinese military headquarters where there was a proper stage and lighting.

It was only on the Chinese instigation of "special" security measures that suspicion was aroused. The general had suggested that the Dalai Lama come alone, or with one or two unarmed bodyguards, so that the visit might remain secret. This was a somewhat ludicrous proposition because Tibetan concern for the Dalai Lama's safety meant there were many people who made it their business to know where he was at all times. As the news of the invitation spread, many Tibetan people decided that it was a plot to kidnap, or even assassinate, the Dalai Lama.

People started to gather around the Norbulingka, and as the crowd swelled so did anti-Chinese feeling. There was a meeting between senior Tibetan and Chinese officials, which degenerated to the extent that the enraged Chinese accused the Tibetans of inciting the crowds and threatened terrible reprisals. They then suggested that the Dalai Lama go to the military headquarters for his own safety and indicated that they would fire at the crowd and the Norbulingka, but the Dalai Lama was able to stall this idea temporarily.

The situation was now desperate, so the Dalai Lama consulted the Nechung Oracle for advice. Previously, the oracle had said that he should remain in Lhasa, but this time as Dorje Drakden took over the medium's body there was a sense of urgency.

> *To my astonishment he shouted, "Go! Go! Tonight!" The medium, still in his trance, then staggered forward, and, snatching up some paper and a pen, wrote down quite clearly and explicitly the route I should take out of the Norbulingka, down to the last Tibetan town on the Indian border. His directions were not what might have been expected.*
>
> 14TH DALAI LAMA

The Dalai Lama performed another ceremony, called a mo, to confirm the oracle's decision, since the chances of a successful escape were by now diminishing rapidly. This was also perhaps the most important decision he would ever have to make. The

Below: The Dalai Lama with the Nechung Oracle in a trance, being supported by attendants

mo confirmed the oracle, and an escape plan was immediately put into action. A party of the Dalai Lama's closest advisors, tutors, and family members prepared to leave that very night. A secret meeting was held with the leaders of the crowd outside the Norbulingka, who assured them of a safe passage that evening, since there would be spies among the crowd. Impromptu disguises were hastily put together and provisions gathered for the journey, but almost everything would have to be left behind.

Before leaving, the Dalai Lama went to the shrine room of Mahakala, his personal protector deity, to say his prayers. There were some monks already there performing puja – religious ritual – and saying prayers. He read a passage from the Buddhist scriptures in which Buddha spoke of the need for courage and confidence and spent some time in silent meditation.

I went forward and presented a kata, a length of white silk, to the divinity. This is the traditional Tibetan gesture on departure and signifies not only propitiation, but also implies the intention of return.

14TH DALAI LAMA

He then took an old thangka of Palden Lhamo, the female protector deity of Tibet, that had belonged to the 2nd Dalai Lama and went outside for the last time.

FLEEING TO INDIA

Dressed in unfamiliar trousers and a coat, the Dalai Lama was met by similarly disguised officials at one of the gates to the Norbulingka. Under the pretext of conducting a routine tour of inspection, they made their way through the crowds to the Kyichu River. There they were met by men in coracle-style boats,

who ferried them across the river. The Dalai Lama remembers fearing that the noise of the splashing oars would bring either Chinese soldiers or gunfire upon them. On the other side, he was reunited with the rest of his family and entourage and was introduced to the freedom fighters on ponies who were to escort them.

That first night was the most dangerous with high chances of being caught by Chinese soldiers, so the refugees rode almost without a break till daylight. The worst of the danger over, the Dalai Lama recalls the mix-up of their riding animals and equipment.

Because the monastery that had provided the animals had had almost no warning, and because of the dark, the best of them had been fitted with the worst saddles and given to the wrong people, whereas some of the oldest and shaggiest mules wore the finest harnesses and were being ridden by the most senior officials!

The Dalai Lama had originally intended to stay in Tibet and to negotiate with the Chinese at a safe

Above: The Dalai Lama (on the white horse) crossing the Himalayas on his way to exile in India

distance from Lhasa, but during the party's flight, it received news of the shelling of the Norbulingka, fighting, and thousands of deaths. Finally, on March 24, the Dalai Lama, listening on short-wave radio, heard Zhou Enlai announce the dissolution of the Tibetan government. Various groups of freedom-fighters also brought news of the Chinese attempts to close the border and prevent his escape. Thus he came to the sad conclusion that negotiation was no longer possible.

The journey was long and arduous, across some of Tibet's hardest terrain, which was still covered with winter snow. Accommodation was basic and, after one night spent near the border in a tent that leaked, the Dalai Lama succumbed to a bout of dysentery. The group rested for a day at Mangmang but warned that the Chinese were approaching, decided to try to make

Below: The Dalai Lama seen riding a Tibetan dzomo, or female yak, similar to one he rode during his escape

it to the border, despite his illness. An advance party had already been sent to India to ask permission for them to seek asylum, which had been granted.

I now had the difficult task of saying goodbye to the soldiers and freedom-fighters who had escorted me all the way from Lhasa, and who were now about to turn and face the Chinese. After bidding these people a tearful farewell, I was helped on to the broad back of a dzomo [a female hybrid of a yak bull and a common cow], for I was still too ill to ride a horse. And it was on this humble form of transport that I left my native land.

14TH DALAI LAMA

At around 4 p.m. on March 31, 1959, the Dalai Lama dismounted, walked across a clearing in no-man's land, and was greeted by a Gurkha commander bearing a traditional white scarf. He accepted the scarf and stepped across the Indian border and into exile.

A NEW LIFE

Nearly forty years later the Dalai Lama still lives in exile, only a few days' travel from where he first arrived in India. McLeod Ganj, in Himachal Pradesh, is now his home, as well as that of a community of Tibetans who have also made the long trek to freedom. Nowadays tourists flock here, drawn by their interest in Tibetan Buddhism and culture, and above all in the Dalai Lama, this small town's most famous resident. However, settling here was not his original plan when he first arrived in India. He had no idea that his stay would last so long.

Over the years, it has become apparent that there is no prospect of an imminent return to Tibet, despite the Dalai Lama's concerted efforts to negotiate with

the Chinese. So he has adjusted to this new life, which is very different from that of his predecessors who ruled in old Tibet. Unlike his ancestors he is frequently away, visiting the many countries whose Tibetan and Buddhist organizations invite him, but he enjoys his surprisingly simple way of life when at home in McLeod Ganj.

A SIMPLE BUDDHIST MONK

As a Buddhist monk, my concern extends to all members of the human family, and indeed to all suffering sentient beings.

14TH DALAI LAMA

The Dalai Lama has often been heard to say that he is a simple Buddhist monk, and when away from the high-profile international visits and the affairs of the Tibetan government in exile, this is the role that he is happiest to play. He endeavors to spend at least five-and-a-half hours a day engaged in meditation, prayer, and reading scriptures, though these activities are not separate from the other aspects of his life. While eating, for example, he often studies a religious text and the Buddhist scriptures list particular prayers that a practitioner can say for most activities of daily life. As the Dalai Lama spends quite a lot of time traveling, he also prays while doing so.

I have three main reasons for doing so: firstly, it contributes toward fulfillment of my daily duty; secondly, it helps pass the time productively; thirdly, it assuages fear!

14TH DALAI LAMA

On a normal day, the Dalai Lama gets up at around 4 a.m. and starts the day with reciting mantras. He does not drink tea first thing, though this is a thoroughly Tibetan custom in which many other monks indulge, but instead takes Tibetan medicine with hot water. More spiritual practice follows, including prostrations. These are sometimes misunderstood as bowing down to graven images, but are practiced in front of a Buddha statue with the motivation of cultivating Buddhahood in oneself. The Dalai Lama also mentions that they are a good form of exercise!

The Dalai Lama then usually walks in the early morning light, saying prayers and listening to the songs of the birds' dawn chorus. Fond of watching birds, he has positioned a bird feeder near the window of one of his main rooms. Over breakfast, he might listen to the news on the BBC's "World Service," or simply read a religious text, before undertaking a period of meditation for a couple of hours. This is followed by studying Buddhist philosophy till lunch.

His afternoon is taken up with government work, giving audiences and interviews, and performing other official duties. Dinner is eaten at around 6 p.m., after which he might watch a little television or read a

Left: The Dalai Lama arrives in India after his escape from Tibet, 1959

Right: Two men crossing the Kyichu River, Lhasa, in a yakskin boat

Far right: A montage showing a photograph of the young Dalai Lama's face placed on a painting, 1958

newspaper before finishing his day with more prayer and meditation. He retires at around 9 p.m. and reports that he usually sleeps quickly and deeply. Though there are fewer and fewer of these simple days, he welcomes the burgeoning interest in Tibetan Buddhism. One has only to attend a teaching session by the Dalai Lama to see how much he enjoys sharing his profound knowledge of Buddhism.

Science is also a subject that fascinates the Dalai Lama. He has met with various leading scientific professionals and has participated in several conferences examining the close links between spirituality and science. He feels that these links are vital to comprehend fully how our world exists, and that this understanding will lead to a greater respect for the natural world. He often speaks about the fragility of the planet's ecology. He has also encouraged scientific studies on the changes that occur in brainwaves when a person enters a state of deep meditation, and these have proved useful in developing an understanding of how our minds work.

For a couple of weeks a year the Dalai Lama breaks his routine to undertake a meditation retreat. He has said that he would like to spend three years in retreat but realizes how difficult this would be, given the demands on his time. While on retreat, he will spend up to twelve hours a day engaged in spiritual practice, and this provides a welcome break from his official duties and giving audiences. Yet the essence of being a "simple Buddhist monk" is to help others find happiness and avoid suffering, and through the public teachings and talks that he gives, he profoundly touches the lives of many people around the world, sharing with them the ancient spiritual philosophies that enable us all to find happiness.

A Man of Peace

The presentation of the Nobel Peace Prize to the Dalai Lama took place on December 10, 1989, which is the birthday of the United Nations' Declaration of Human Rights. The following extracts and comments are taken from speeches and interviews at the ceremony.

You are a man now recognized all over the world as one of the most prominent spokesmen for human rights as the very foundation for a true, just, and lasting peace. Could anything be more appropriate than to celebrate this today than giving the Peace Prize to you?

EGIL AARVIK,
CHAIRMAN OF THE NOBEL COMMITTEE

I am a simple Buddhist monk from Tibet, someone who follows with deep conviction a spiritual way of life, particularly the noble path of the Buddha, the essence of which is the skillful unification of universal compassion and wisdom. I am also someone who, through a natural course of events, is linked to the fate of Tibet, its people, and culture, and who has dedicated all his energy in fulfilling this responsibility. That such a person has been awarded the Nobel Peace Prize is indeed a great honor. I feel a great joy and a sense of pride. And I am certain that for people all over the world who truly believe in, and aspire toward, world peace and genuine harmony, this award will also be a source of joy.

Therefore I would like to express to everyone my sincere thanks. This award represents worldwide recognition and support for the just cause of the Tibetan people's struggle for freedom and self-determination… And just as I hope and pray every day for an enduring peace on our planet, I will also work hard toward this goal so that a day may dawn when people all over the world will love and help each other and live in genuine harmony.

14TH DALAI LAMA

I am so happy, I came all the way to Oslo to see him receive it. This has been a fantastic day for His Holiness, for Tibetan people, but especially for peace in this world.

CHARLES ROSE, U.S. CONGRESSMAN

I feel the Dalai Lama is one of the very few individuals as a male leader, one of a very few soft and also feminist-thinking, ecological, and decentralized-thinking leaders. There are very few in

Below: The Dalai Lama greeting Indian visitors, 1989

the world. That's why the doors are closing on him, because the language he is speaking, the spirituality he has, is not understood by the materialistic people, and it is not understood by the Chinese because the materialistic philosophy in their government can't cope with the spirituality of the Dalai Lama. I think that the Dalai Lama is probably the most political and most effective in bringing across that nonviolence is the only solution in the atomic age.

PETRA KELLY, WEST GERMAN MP

✦

I was very happy when it happened. I think it has been a great encouragement, not only for Tibet and the struggle for human rights and freedom for Tibet, and also a great achievement for the Dalai Lama, but I think it is a great encouragement for the struggle for human rights and dignity throughout the world.

HARALD ELEFSEN, NORWEGIAN MP

✦

The committee wants to emphasize the fact that the Dalai Lama, in his struggle for the liberation of Tibet, consistently has opposed the use of violence. He has instead advocated peaceful solutions based upon tolerance and mutual respect in order to preserve the historical and cultural heritage of his people. In the opinion of the committee the Dalai Lama has come forward with constructive and forward-looking proposals for the solution of international conflicts, human-rights issues, and global environmental problems.

NORWEGIAN NOBEL COMMITTEE,
DECEMBER, 1989

Left: Giving a Kalachakra blessing for world peace at Jispa, northern India, 1994

As soon as I heard about this prize, my mind's first thought was, I want to do something for those people on this same planet who are facing starvation. So I want to contribute some portion of this money to projects for hunger. Secondly, I very much want to contribute; you see, in India there are some organizations that look after lepers and on a few occasions I made some small contribution. So now, I want to contribute some money from this to that project.

Then another thing: I want to contribute to one of those existing institutions that make an effort for world peace. Then another portion for some Tibetan institution, mainly in education, I want to use some money. Then I want to establish a foundation, a Tibetan Foundation for Universal Responsibility. So these are my aims.

14TH DALAI LAMA

7

~

The Dalai Lama as an International Figure

So far, I have received only support for my belief that wherever you go,

people everywhere are basically the same, despite certain superficial differences.

14TH DALAI LAMA

Main picture: At the Kalachakra initiation that the Dalai Lama gave in Mongolia in 1995, during his first visit there since the demise of the Soviet Union

Right: The Dalai Lama greeting members of the audience at the Royal Albert Hall, London, 1984

ews of the Tibetan occupation and of the Dalai Lama's exile in India might not have produced any political intervention, but it did generate an esoteric interest internationally. This continued to develop over the years, and individuals and small groups started to explore ways of addressing the situation in Tibet and

helping the Tibetans. But most of all, the Dalai Lama, as a Buddhist monk and teacher, an advocate of peace and compassion, as well as the leader of Tibet, increasingly captured the imagination and hearts of thousands of people around the world.

During the first years of his exile, other than his earlier visit to China, the Dalai Lama had not visited any countries except for India, where he now lived, but in 1967 he took his first trip abroad, visiting Japan and Thailand. He met mainly with other Buddhist monastics on this occasion, which he enjoyed a great deal, because he felt that this helped him see Tibetan Buddhism in the larger Buddhist context and realize how well Buddhism travels to other countries, in that religious practices are basically the same, despite a few cultural differences. However, the thorny problem also arose as to the role in which he should be invited to these countries in order not to compromise the country concerned in its diplomatic and trade relationships with China.

The Chinese government subsequently attempted to prevent the Dalai Lama from engaging in any formal meetings with foreign government officials, saying that this would be construed as intervention in its internal affairs. This edict is still in place today, which means that when the Dalai Lama visits another country, it is as a religious teacher, or conference delegate, or spokesperson on peace. Since the Tibetan government in exile is not recognized by the majority of the countries that he visits, he cannot discuss anything political with foreign government officials, and often does not meet them publicly unless that country's leading religious figure is also present. He

Below: The Dalai Lama with Heinrich Harrer at the opening of Harrer's photographic exhibition to celebrate the International Year of Tibet, New York, 1990

has, however, met both Bill Clinton and John Major socially or during informal drop-in visits. This has not diminished the number of invitations extended to him, however, or the Dalai Lama's enthusiasm to meet many different people.

Especially, I welcome the opportunity offered by travel to meet and talk with people from all walks of life – some poor, some rich, some well educated, some ill educated, some who are religious, many who are not.

14TH DALAI LAMA

VISITING EUROPE

For six weeks in 1973, the Dalai Lama toured Europe, visiting eleven countries and encountering Western cultures for the first time. Thrilled at the opportunity to discover in person the European cities that he had previously seen only in picture books, he was also curious about the cultural differences between East and West. Yet he recalls that on flying into Rome – the first stop on his tour – his first impression was of seeing the same trees and signs of human habitation that were already familiar to him and noted that any differences were, therefore, only superficial.

In Rome, he met Pope Paul VI and was delighted to find that they agreed on the importance of religious belief, whatever the creed. He renewed his acquaintance with Heinrich Harrer and found it a great pleasure to see his old friend again. In Switzerland, he met some of the two hundred children, early Tibetan exiles who had been adopted by Swiss families. This was a deeply moving experience for the Dalai Lama, but it was also one tinged with sadness since most of them could no longer speak Tibetan.

Left: The Dalai Lama being welcomed by crowds of well-wishers in Poland

Though it was a whirlwind tour, with never enough time to gain more than a surface impression of the many places that he visited, this first international trip was an exciting and amazing experience for the Dalai Lama. This first visit to Europe also stimulated widespread interest in Tibet and Tibetan Buddhsim, resulting in many further invitations.

Everywhere I went I found the same kindness and hospitality and thirst for information about Tibet. It became clear to me that my country holds a special fascination for many people around the world.

14TH DALAI LAMA

HELLO DALAI!

Finally, in 1979, the Dalai Lama visited the United States, mindful of its reputation as the richest and freest country in the world. He was greeted by the *New York Times* front-page headline, "Hello Dalai!" which amusingly marked this encounter. Although he had already visited Europe, and had thus experienced any initial culture shock between East and West, the United States is perhaps the touchstone of modern Western cultural values and the standard by which they are judged. Therefore this visit to the United States was a particularly interesting and thought-provoking experience for the Dalai Lama.

Inevitably influenced by the Chinese propaganda against capitalism to which he had been exposed during his time in China, the Dalai Lama was now able to ascertain for himself if there was any truth in the rhetoric to which he had listened. His first impressions were favorable; people seemed free to express themselves without censure, both verbally and in terms of their lifestyles. He found everyone whom he met to be open and friendly, and interested in hearing about himself and Tibet. He was received warmly wherever he spoke – even though he felt that his English was poor – and he enjoyed the youthful enthusiasm of the student audiences that he addressed.

However, he also noticed some things that surprised him and that lent some credibility to the communist critique. He was amazed to see beggars in such a prosperous country and was disturbed by the inequality of living standards, with both rich and destitute people mingling on the streets of the big cities. He observed that wealth, and the earning of it, produced stress and anxiety, and that people needed to take tranquilizers to help them sleep. He also found that the cult of the individual, which freed people from the restraints of family and class to some degree, also resulted in alienation and loneliness. And the much admired (by Westerners) freedom of thought sometimes produced an "either–or" mentality, which tended to ignore relativity and shades of gray between absolutes.

Now, as I have come to know the country better, I have begun to see that in some ways the American political system does not live up to its own ideals.

14TH DALAI LAMA

But there is much that the Dalai Lama admires about the United States, and he has chosen to deliver some of his biggest public teaching sessions there, particularly the Kalachakra initiation at New York's Madison Square Garden in 1992. The United States is home to many Buddhist centers and practitioners; funds seem easier to raise for projects there, and enthusiasm and dedication characterize the Tibetan Buddhist scene in America.

The Dalai Lama's overall impression of the West firmly convinced him that democracy was a good thing, and this has led to many of the changes made to the Tibetan government in exile, which is now run on democratic principles. Having witnessed both communist and capitalist extremes, the Dalai Lama concluded that a middle-way approach, drawing from both systems, was the most likely to bring both material prosperity and happiness. The cultural exchange that has occurred during his tours has also

Below: Giving another Kalachakra initiation in Madison, Wisconsin, in 1979

influenced those Western people who are dissatisfied with materialism and greed, and the United States and Europe now boast an increasing number of Buddhist communities. These communities offer a positive and structured alternative to mainstream Western culture, and gradually their values are beginning to have an influence on their societies.

WINNING THE NOBEL PEACE PRIZE

In 1989 the Nobel Committee awarded its prize for peace to the Dalai Lama. This award gave international recognition to his peaceful efforts to resolve the situation in Tibet, as well as enabling him to reach a wider audience. Support for the Tibetans increased as a result, and many new Tibet support groups sprang up around the world. Interest in the Dalai Lama himself also grew through the prominence and authority of the Nobel platform. Many were touched by his spontaneous generosity and warmth, as well as his serious concern for his country and its people.

Left: The Dalai Lama at a conference on global survival, in Oxford, England

I am very happy to be here with you today to receive the Nobel prize for peace. I feel great honor, [and I am] humbled and greatly moved that you should give this prize to a simple Buddhist monk of Tibet. I am no one special, but I believe the prize is a recognition of the true value of altruism, love, compassion, and nonviolence, which I try to practice in accordance with the teachings of the Buddha and the great sages of India and Tibet. I accept the prize with profound gratitude on behalf of the oppressed everywhere and for all those who struggle for freedom and world peace [and] as a tribute to the man who founded the modern tradition of nonviolent action for change, Mahatma Gandhi, whose life taught and inspired me. And of course I accept it on behalf of the six million Tibetan people, my brave countrymen and women inside Tibet, who have suffered and continue to suffer so much. They confront a calculated and systematic strategy aimed at the destruction of their national and cultural identities. The prize reaffirms our conviction that with truth, courage, and determination as our weapons, Tibet will be liberated.

14TH DALAI LAMA

THE DALAI LAMA
ON TOUR TODAY

These days, the Dalai Lama receives many more invitations than it is possible for him to accept, and some are regretfully declined. Invitations to give Buddhist teaching sessions or to attend conferences are extended a year or two in advance in order that they may be fitted into his busy schedule. For the lucky ones, his acceptance heralds the start of eighteen months to two years of organization in advance of the momentous occasion. The Dalai Lama's 1996 U.K. tour, in which I played a small part in arranging and for which I organized the video recording, provides a good example.

There were three inviting organizations, which were coordinated by the U.K. Office of Tibet. One of these was the newly formed Network of Buddhist Organisations (N.B.O.) U.K., and there was some initial trepidation about undertaking such a huge endeavor. Nervous questions, such as "Will we be able to recoup our costs through ticket sales?" echoed through the room in which preliminary discussions were held. But the enthusiasm for being part of such

Right: The Dalai Lama at the Camden Centre in London, 1984

a special occasion prevailed, and the N.B.O., along with the Tibet Society and the Buddhist Society, proffered an invitation to the Dalai Lama. This was accepted and initiated months of dedicated hard work.

Large venues were booked; in London, Alexandra Palace for a public talk, a Tibet festival, and an interfaith conference, the Barbican for a Buddhist teaching session on "The Four Noble Truths," and, for those in the north, the Free Trade Hall in Manchester for another public talk. The Buddhist Society – an umbrella organization for Buddhists of all traditions – would host a small event for British Buddhist delegates. A press conference would also be held in the Jubilee Room of the Houses of Parliament, and the Dalai Lama would be accorded the personal touch of tea with the Queen Mother.

As the Dalai Lama's arrival drew close, the tension accelerated. Tickets were as precious as gold dust, and rumors ran wild regarding the best place to stand near the various entrances and exits in order to catch a glimpse of the Dalai Lama, or to have the best chance of receiving a quick blessing and handshake. The day finally came. Tibetans resident in Britain lined the streets wearing traditional clothes and holding white greeting scarves and bundles of burning incense. Security guards kept the crowd back, though the Dalai Lama's arrival was not a public event, and only those "in the know" were there. We positioned our cameras, and everyone waited.

Suddenly the place erupted as the cavalcade of automobiles drew up. Then the Dalai Lama got out of his automobile, smiling and laughing and greeting as many people as he could reach. Those whom he touched were profoundly moved, often dissolving into tears of joy. Just before entering the house in which he

would stay for the duration of his visit, he turned at the top of the steps, smiling when he caught the eyes of people he knew and waving to everyone. Then he went to rest and say his prayers before embarking on his grueling ten-day schedule.

Immediately after dawn, we arrived at Alexandra Palace to spend a few hours setting up our video equipment. The place was already bustling with activity and there was an atmosphere of goodwill and excitement. With the July sunshine filtering through the huge, stained-glass windows, the vast hall slowly filled with thousands of people. Tibetan dancers and singers entertained the expectant crowd. A delay was announced: the Dalai Lama's train had been held up. Good-natured groans echoed around the hall, but everyone waited patiently. Then suddenly he was on the stage, receiving a noisy and heartfelt welcome.

His talk at Alexandra Palace was quite short, not only because of the delay but also because the crowd cheered almost everything that he said, somewhat carried away by its enthusiasm and devotion. Yet the Dalai Lama did not mind at all and accurately pitched the level of his talk to the mood of the crowd, making jokes that had his audience in fits of laughter. Then it was all over, and he was gone. Slowly and happily the people dispersed, and we packed up all our video equipment and moved on to the next venue.

Everywhere the Dalai Lama went he received the same rapturous welcome from serious Buddhists, Tibet supporters, and the many people who simply love and feel inspired by this special person. They are interested in what he has to say and in how they can apply this advice to their daily lives. His wisdom is often humorous, his compassion shines through his presence, and he touches people simply by living

Left: The Dalai Lama teaching the Four Noble Truths at the Barbican Centre, London, in 1996

according to these ideals. When you are in his presence you feel touched by love, and he also generates a sense of peace and inner tranquility amid all the bustle of the roadshow surrounding him.

These are archetypal human qualities, and people the world over are touched in the same way. There are no barriers of nationality, age, culture, or religious belief inherent in how the Dalai Lama is and what he teaches. Almost everyone he meets is full of gratitude for the good fortune that brought them their encounter with this remarkable man. He is truly an international spokesperson for the ancient wisdom that he translates so well in a contemporary world.

8
~

An Interview with the Dalai Lama

On July 4, 1996, I walked along one of the two main streets of McLeod Ganj toward

the Dalai Lama's palace for our interview. The air that afternoon was heavy and humid, with early monsoon

rain threatening to fall, and I was glad to arrive in an air-conditioned waiting room following the security

checks, where I composed myself and gathered my thoughts. After a short time, Tenzin Geyche, the Dalai

Lama's private secretary who would act as translator when necessary during the interview, ushered me into a

comfortably furnished and spacious drawing room. The Dalai Lama was already there and after greeting me

warmly and putting me at ease, he suggested that we sit down and start the interview. I gave him a brief

description of the book that I was writing and launched into the first question.

GFH: *Which one message from Buddha's teachings would you like everyone to know and apply?*

DL: Altruism and a good heart, not only to human beings but also other animals – all sentient beings. Whether someone is a believer or a nonbeliever in Buddhism, people caring for ecology, or some individuals and organizations fighting for animal rights and against cruelty to animals, these are very good. Furthermore, I think if we promote an altruistic attitude toward not only oneself, not only humanity, but all other forms of life, then I think our attitude becomes more peaceful, more nonviolent. Also the foundation of secular ethics is good.

GFH: *What do you think about the encounter of Tibetan Buddhism with modern Western society and values?*

DL: I always feel that Buddhism and all major world religions, no doubt about it, deal with basic human suffering and human problems. Particularly Buddhism – this is a way to deal with problems through mental effort. So, as far as basic human emotional problems are concerned, I believe there are no essential differences between Eastern or Western [people]. There are some cultural differences, but as far as the teachings of Buddhism are concerned, people are the same, or similar; [there are] no real differences.

Main picture:
The Dalai Lama
in reflective mood

*Right: The Dalai
Lama in
lighthearted mood*

*Far right:
Answering a
question
emphatically*

Usually when people look to the Buddhist traditions, they look on the basis of art or music and so gain a general impression of a particular religion. Some people might look at the dress that monks of a certain tradition wear and think they have a rough idea of what that religion might be [like].

Then, of course, there are differences. Usually when we hear this word "Buddhism" we immediately think of temples and so on, but if someone visited Milarepa's cave, he would find it was not Buddhist, or Christian – nothing; just an empty cave. Therefore I think Buddhism means the Four Noble Truths [suffering, the causes of suffering, the cessation of suffering, the path to the cessation of suffering] and two truths [conventional reality: how we perceive the world; and ultimate reality: how things truly exist], and it all needs mental effort. In this case it [makes] no difference whether someone is Eastern or Western.

GFH: *Why are you spending an increasing amount of time in the West?*
DL: Only in response to many invitations!

GFH: *Why do you think there is so much interest in the Dalai Lama and Tibetan Buddhism in the West?*
DL: We can't say "Western" in this generalized way. But among the Westerners a number of people are showing an interest in Eastern philosophy and thought. Then [there is] the interest in Buddhism. Here, I feel, firstly there is a tendency to want to know more about something unfamiliar. This is usual; human nature always wants something new, I think. I feel in the West there are always new songs, new dances, new fashions. Similarly, with spirituality, there is a tendency to find something new.

Then, I think, as far as Buddhism is concerned, there is always talk about training the mind, a combination of

faith and wisdom; intelligence and faith combined. That seems to be a new way. Some scholars told me Buddhism in general, and Tibetan Buddhism in particular, nicely combine faith and wisdom. So religious practice using analytical meditation, this is using human intellectual capacity; that's why some Western scholars really show appreciation.

Then meditation, of course, is not only for Buddhists, but for many human beings. In ancient Christian practice, meditation was also important, but later decreased, I think. Some Christian brothers and sisters are also now showing a keen interest in meditation. So that, I feel, is very good; to remain as a Christian, but to be able to adopt some technical methods still available in other traditions. That, I think, is the main reason [why there is so much interest in Buddhism in the West]. Especially when serious practitioners see that the Buddhist way and approach mainly uses training of mind – a technique with a lot of ways to improve our good qualities and reduce negativities – I think this is one of the main attractions.

Buddhism is also rational and logical. I have encountered some Christians who felt Christianity was rational and Buddhism not rational; [they spoke of this] not in an argumentative way, [they were] very matter of fact, but this made me feel confused! [laughs] Really serious practitioners who get some different experiences through meditation, then find their appreciation of meditation increases.

GFH: *What do you think of the films currently being made about you?*
DL: Personally, I do not have much feeling. But regarding more awareness about Tibet then these films are certainly very useful. Among the people who are involved in making these two films there are those who have some feelings for the Tibetans. They are supporting these films enthusiastically because they feel this will be a good thing for Tibetans. It seems to me they are not thinking about money, but I think some kind of moral principle is there, so I feel very happy.

I have seen a kind of trailer on the film about my life story, so when I saw the young boys who are acting as the Dalai Lama – in fact there are three of them – I felt that when I was young I was much brighter than these boys! [much laughter] The scenery is all artificially created sets; these are really remarkable, really expert.

GFH: *Which leading world figures do you admire, and why?*
DL: First, Chairman Mao! [laughs] No really, some aspects of Mao made him a great leader. I also learned some useful advice from him. Of course, as time passed, other, more negative, aspects became clear. Some other Chinese leaders were also impressive when I was in China in 1945. Then in India, 1956, the first Indian president [Dr. Rajendra Prasad] was a great leader. I'm not sure if he was known as a world statesman, but I respected him greatly. Nehru in one aspect was a great leader, and in one aspect more Western than Indian.

Among Western leaders I have met, Willy Brandt was, I think, something. Of people still alive, Vaclav Havel, though I have [heard] some criticism recently. Then, of course, Nelson Mandela. Up to [his] becoming president I have some admiration, then after I have even more admiration. He really cares very distinctly about the spirit of reconciliation. Quite remarkable. John Major, when I look at his face, he seems very beautiful, very nice. Of course, I don't know his policies well enough, but I liked him as a person when I met him. Then my recent meeting with the Taiwanese president, Lee Teng-hui; firstly, regarding Chinese history, he is quite an expert. Also he is the first-ever popularly elected president in 5,000 years of Chinese history. He has a very spiritual mind, which impressed me, showing me his eagerness to learn and practice spirituality. I think in terms of Christianity he really has strong feelings.

GFH: *You are in favor of interfaith dialog; what do you feel this achieves?*

DL: Closer understanding, and a positive impression to the public also. Another thing is the meeting and exchange of spiritual experience. Extremely useful. I myself certainly learn the value of Buddhist effectiveness by looking at different traditions. As a result, I acknowledge, and have admiration and recognition, that all different major world religions are equally very useful. So I have much respect [for these religions]. As a result of our contact, some of our brothers and sisters in other religious traditions have some positive and more open attitude, I think. I feel quite proud I made some contribution in this respect.

Also in my efforts I do not attempt to propagate Buddhadharma [teachings of Buddha]. My basic attitude is how much Buddhism can contribute, not how to propagate it. So when I explain or teach Buddhism to Westerners, or Hindus, or those from a non-Buddhist background, then I hesitate; when they come for a public audience I do not give them blessed pills, but I am worried that some of them may feel [the] Dalai Lama is discriminating, and only giving [them] to Tibetans, not Westerners! [laughs] If I know someone is a Buddhist practitioner then I give,

otherwise I feel [a] sacred pill, which is blessed according to the Buddhist tradition, is something very sacred, so it is not correct and proper to give to non-Buddhists.

This is the same for all sacred things in all traditions. If I was in a Christian church and the priest offered me holy communion, I am afraid I would not feel very comfortable! Of course, I have very much respect for Jesus Christ and Christian tradition, but I also feel you need to believe in these things – very important. So I have respect for these different religious traditions because they are right for many people, this is self-evident, but this does not mean these other traditions are right for me.

GFH: *Which memories are clearest today from the time you lived in Tibet?*

DL: Some happy moments, some frightening moments. I always enjoyed leaving the Potala and going to the summer palace, Norbulingka, at the official start of summer. The season was most beautiful, all the lawns were turning green, the apricot trees flowering and the birds singing. In May, 1993, during my U.K. tour, I visited Wales for the first time. Very beautiful countryside. In front of the castle [Cardiff] were some peacocks. This reminded me of my own palace in Lhasa. When I left in March, 1959, some peacocks were there, so I always have some kind of concern, some feeling [about] what happened to them after I left.

GFH: *In a recent statement you said if the Tibetan issue remains unresolved and the Tibetans still want a Dalai Lama you would reincarnate outside Tibet. What are the implications of this?*

DL: For many years I have said this. This recent statement was in a specific context, I can explain later.

In any case, if, during my lifetime, the return to Tibet does not materialize, the Tibetan people want me to continue, and I pass away outside Tibet as a refugee, then logically if it is wanted the reincarnation will appear outside. Because the purpose of the reincarnation is to continue the tasks started by the previous life which have not yet been accomplished. So in my lifetime as 14th Dalai Lama I started some work, like the freedom struggle, which is not yet fulfilled, so the task of the next reincarnation is to continue that work.

So, if the next reincarnation comes inside Tibet, and in case the Chinese manipulate that situation, then this becomes the destroyer of the work started by the 14th Dalai Lama. Then, politically, some Chinese officials have expressed that the whole Tibetan issue very much relies on one person. That person is now getting older and older and once that person has passed away, we will choose another young Dalai Lama. Then there will be no future for the Tibetan struggle. This happened as early as the 1980s, so this is a foolish calculation by these Chinese officials. So therefore, politically, I felt it is necessary to make the issue clear in case this happens.

GFH: *How do you reconcile the different approaches of modern science and practices such as the oracle and throwing mos?*

DL: Science accepts definition. I think, according to my understanding, science is mainly dealing with reality, including the physical aspect. Up till now it has been focused mainly on the physical, things which have a foundation. But like consciousness, or some other abstract thing, these you cannot calculate or measure, but they also exist. So now, like the oracle is

Left: Happy memories for the Dalai Lama include summers at Norbulingka

a different form of life I believe exists, not only human beings or animals, but different forms of life are certainly there. We cannot state only those things we can experience exist and all the things we cannot experience do not exist. This we cannot say. In the nineteenth century, scientists at that time stated certain things existed and beyond that was nonexistence. Now, in the twentieth century, we find many more things that exist. Again, [as] we find things on this same basis we cannot say nothing else exists, and in the next century we will find more new phenomena also.

So therefore I firmly believe the field of science can expand later in the future. Up to now the view of science has seen oracles and so on as something mysterious, hasn't it? So from that level, of course, there is a contradiction. But to me science is limited, with more to learn. Therefore from that perspective I do not see any contradiction.

GFH: *What are your feelings and advice about the practice of tantra [a Buddhist meditation practice known as the quick path to enlightenment]?*
DL: Among the Tibetan community, generally speaking there is too much practice of tantra. Of the

Above: The Dalai Lama holding a damaru drum

three generations of Tibetans here now [in India], the majority are Buddhist since they were young children, some kind of faith is there, learned from their parents and family. Even then, too much. Generally, the majority of Tibetans in their daily practice include some form of Vajrayana [tantra] practice. Certainly this practice is without proper foundation. That is clear.

Like the followers of Atisha about eight hundred years ago, some tantric masters never show people they practice tantrayana. Nowadays, in the monasteries some young monks recite poorly these tantric sadhanas [prayers including visualization] without knowing anything. So I think unfortunately this is how it is. So, in one way the Buddhist community is very good, but in another way the practices are superficial and not properly done.

Westerners have a different background and tradition, but also have an interest in tantrayana. You should practice the Four Noble Truths and the two truths, then study and practice. Once you gain some experience about altruism, some understanding about sunyata [emptiness; the philosophy that nothing exists by itself and that all things are interdependent], then eventually you can start the practice of tantrayana. That is the proper way. If we truly study Buddhadharma sincerely, then this is step by step. If we take Buddhadharma at an academic and intellectual level, that's alright, you can study everything.

In our mind, unless we go through step by step, it is unrealistic. Some Westerners ask me which is the quickest method; if you read about tantra it is described as the quickest and best. That does not mean quickest for everyone. It means for those people who are fully prepared, who have done the groundwork, that it is right. Now, if you ask which university is best,

you can say this university is best for a certain subject like technology. That does not mean automatically all children should join there because it is best. It is best only for those students who already have all the background for the study. Similarly, for those who have done all the preparations, the best practice is tantra. That's really important, I feel, in many respects.

I have many anxieties as to how Tibetans themselves are practicing Buddhism, so naturally I also have a great deal of anxiety about Westerners. So I am not discouraging our Western Buddhists from practicing tantrayana, but you should do all the preparations, all the preliminary practices and study, beforehand.

The true meaning of nectar [a divine offering to the Buddhas, normally visualized or substituted by saffron water or alcohol in ceremonies] is "dirty substances transformed into something you can taste as nectar." I can't do this, but Naropa received some dirty thing from Tilopa and this happened. So, the proper way is to have some deeper experience and realization. Then to test this exercise is good.

Likewise with sexual practices. Some sex scandals also happening now, very unfortunate. One ancient Indian master told his student, until you reach a certain stage you should remain as a monk. Later he told him, even if he was able to make a fruit on a tree fall down through the power of his meditation, it is still not time to disrobe. Only when you can also make the fruit go back on the tree is it time for these practices. The reason is tantric practices work with the subtle energies moving up and down the chakras. In reality these sexual practices are not sexual intercourse, even though they look like it. So therefore tantric practice is quite dangerous and risky. It can easily be misunderstood, so one must be careful.

GFH: *How do you meditate?*

DL: Usually four hours in the morning and one-and-a-half hours in the evening, so altogether five or six hours. Then formal meditation, the major portion is recitation. This is something like a revision or reminding yourself of the practices. Some recitation is reciting mantras, or saying some prayers or praises to Buddha; these are just recitation. The rest are words you recite as a reminder for realization and analytical meditation. Those words remind you of the practices you need to do, so they are not just reciting mantras or praises, they are actual practice. Then my main practice is practice of altruism, impermanence, bodhicitta [the altruistic aspiration to help all beings reach enlightenment], and emptiness. These are the major points in my practice.

Good, thank you!

Below: Pictured with President Nelson Mandela, South Africa, 1996

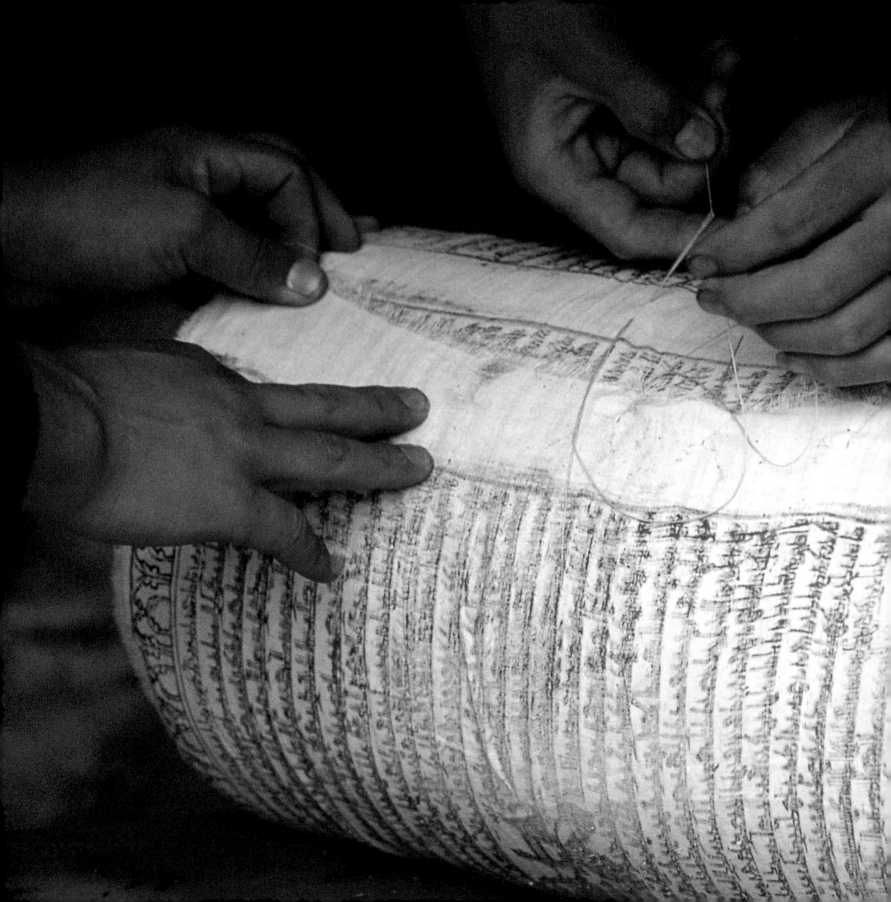

part three

~

TIBETAN
BUDDHISM

9
~

An Introduction
to Tibetan Buddhism

Tibetan Buddhism comprises one of several developments from the Buddha's original teachings. Other

schools arose in Sri Lanka, Thailand, and Burma, and became known as the Theravadan traditions.

Buddha's teachings also traveled to Japan, China, Vietnam, and Korea, where Zen Buddhism flowered.

Previous pages: from left: Prayers and mantras being stitched into a roll for placing inside a prayer wheel; a Tibetan nomad girl; members of the Tibetan Institute of Performing Arts

Right: The distribution of offerings at Bodhgaya, India

Far right: A pilgrim saying prayers beneath the Bodhi tree

These days, Buddhism is still traveling, this time to the West, where, over time, the teachings from the existing schools will transform into an appropriate Western tradition. So, to understand Tibetan Buddhism in the wider context, we need to look at its origins; the life and teachings of Shakyamuni Buddha, the founder of Buddhism.

Prince Siddhartha Gautama was born around six hundred years before Jesus Christ, in a small kingdom lying in the foothills of the Himalayas, near the border between India and Nepal. His father – King Shuddhodana, the head of the Shakya clan – was pleased to have produced a son and heir, and naturally assumed that Siddhartha would succeed him as king on his death. However, at the feast held to celebrate the child's birth, a holy man named Asita who was renowned for his predictive powers, was asked to bless Siddhartha. Gazing upon the baby's face, Asita immediately realized that he was seeing a great religious teacher and was deeply moved.

Shuddhodana became concerned about Asita's obvious emotion and reverence and ordered him to make his pronouncement at once. Swiftly realizing that the king would not take kindly to the fact that his son would end up renouncing his birthright, Asita foretold that Siddhartha would either be a great king or a religious leader, hoping that this ambiguity would

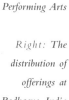

Buddhism is more than an Asian religion.

14TH DALAI LAMA

Far right: Jowo Buddha statue in the Jokhang, Lhasa – the most revered statue in Tibet and reputed to have been blessed by Shakyamuni Buddha

Below far right: Buddha statue with a kata (white silk scarf) offering

pacify the king. Shuddhodana did not fall for this ruse, however, and immediately banished Asita from his kingdom. Realizing that it would be the hardships of life that would turn his son toward religion, he decided to create a pleasure dome inside the palace walls that his son would never leave.

Siddhartha grew up surrounded by everything that was beautiful and luxurious; his every need was catered for before it even arose. The palace was a paradise for the senses, and anything unpleasant or ugly was banned. The only thing that was denied him by his otherwise indulgent father was a glimpse of the outside world, but until he was in his late twenties, Siddhartha was not unduly bothered by this. At this time, he finally grew bored of luxurious and sensual indulgence, and even his beautiful wife and baby son were no consolation. So his father staged a massive clean-up in the immediate vicinity of the palace and then permitted Siddhartha three trips into town.

But even the powerful king could not completely hold back the harsh, fundamental realities of life, and Siddhartha saw an old person, a sick person, and a corpse. Questioning his servants, he discovered that all beings are subject to birth, sickness, old age, and death – even himself. This news plunged him into existential despair, and he sat by the river, head in hands, contemplating the suffering of existence. Then he saw a holy man who had no possessions and was wearing only rags, yet he was radiant with contentment and seemingly unbothered by his poverty. "This is the answer to all this awful suffering," thought Siddhartha, and decided to embark upon the religious life.

That night he fled from the palace, cut off his hair, cast off his fine clothes, and started his spiritual journey. He sought out the great holy men of the day and spent time with them, learning as much as he could. Still unsatisfied, he performed various meditations and finally ended up in the forest with some fellow seekers of truth, practicing extreme asceticism. Still wrestling with desire, and near starvation, he wandered toward the river. There he met a girl tending cows, who offered him a dish of milk and rice. He accepted, and as the nourishment filled his body, he realized that asceticism was not the answer any more than sensual indulgence had been, and that a middle-way approach was best.

His friends scornfully abandoned him, saying that he had given up, so Siddhartha decided to sit in meditation under a peepul tree until he found the answers that he was looking for. He entered a deep meditation and watched the demons of desire and ignorance of how things really exist dance before him, but he remained unmoved. As the dawn light filtered through the leaves, he saw the world with new eyes, beyond the duality of pleasure and suffering, life and death. Siddhartha had become enlightened and had entered a state of Nirvana.

Right: A monk in Nepal holds a rosary and a photograph of the Dalai Lama

Main picture:
Thangka depicting
Buddha and the
sixteen Arhats

Above: Chenrezig
statue with kata

Left: Guru
Rinpoche statue in
the Jokhang, 1994

Main picture:
A Tibetan woman
pilgrim gazing at
the Buddha Rock
on the Lingkor, the
circumambulation
route around Lhasa

THE BUDDHIST WAY

The fundamental precept of Buddhism is interdependence, or the law of cause and effect. This simply states that everything an individual being experiences is derived through action from motivation.

14TH DALAI LAMA

The Buddha, as Siddhartha had now become, spent the rest of his life teaching and ordaining those who chose a monastic way of life. He taught only when requested and spent several months of each year in meditational retreat. He deliberately tried not to build up a cult or rigid religion, preferring instead to be a spiritual friend or guide, who helped individuals to find their own way to enlightenment. He also taught on all levels to suit the varying ability of his listeners and had the gift to present profound truths simply. This ability is reflected in one of the Dalai Lama's favorite sayings: "My religion is kindness."

What does it actually mean to be a Buddhist? This is not the easiest of questions to answer, particularly because "Buddhist" is a recently invented Western word. The Tibetans, and other Asian Buddhists, simply

Right: Prayer
wheels in
Kathmandu, Nepal

follow the teachings of the Buddha. This subtle distinction in language contains a powerful message, which is that Buddhism is how we live our everyday lives, and that "Buddhism" is not a convenient label or intellectual preoccupation.

Have courage. Be awake and aware. Remember too that Buddhism is not about being "a Buddhist"; that is, obtaining a new identity tag. Nor is it about collecting head-knowledge, practices, and techniques. It is ultimately about letting go of all forms and concepts and becoming free.

JOHN SNELLING

Having said that, there is, of course, a conventional definition of what it means to be a Buddhist! This is someone who takes refuge in the Three Jewels of Buddha, Dharma, and Sangha. Taking refuge involves trusting, making a commitment, and finding a safe place to which to return, when the world and everything in it, seems chaotic. Buddha is the historical personage, the Shakyamuni Buddha, but the teachings tell us that we should regard our teacher as being inseparable from the Buddha, so that Buddha can also be our teacher, someone like the Dalai Lama. Dharma is the teachings of the Buddha – whether spoken or written – his words of wisdom. And Sangha is the spiritual community. Sometimes Sangha means the monastic community of monks and nuns, but it also means our spiritual friends, who support us just as we offer support to them.

Perhaps the most basic teaching of the Buddha is that of the Four Noble Truths, since it neatly sums up the transformation from samsara to nirvana. Samsara is often pictorially represented as the wheel of life: twelve phases of life and death, six realms of existence,

and the three poisons of ignorance, desire, and aversion that keep us locked into this cycle. The whole wheel is represented as being clutched in the arms of the demon Mara, or illusion. Nirvana is the cessation of birth and death, escaping from the wheel of life by reaching enlightenment. However, this state is not separate from who we are now, but who we really are underneath when we pull the veils of illusion from our eyes.

The First Noble Truth is the recognition that the nature of life is unsatisfactory. We experience pain and death; things, people, or circumstances that we like go away, and those that we don't like come to us; and we have no real control over this ceaseless changing. The Second Noble Truth points out that the cause of this frustration is not inherent in the nature of our unsatisfactory world, but in our reaction to it. Our suffering is actually derived from craving that which we do not have, and hating that which we do have, rather than from the things themselves. The consolation of knowing that there is a way out of this imperfect way of life is the Third Noble Truth, and the Fourth offers a path to achieve this way out, which is based on changing our attitudes and behavior by examining them and realizing that they are based on confusion and misperception.

Above: Jamyang Khyentse Chokyi Lodro

Below: Dilgo Khyentse Rinpoche

THE DEVELOPMENT OF TIBETAN BUDDHISM

In every culture where Buddhism has spread, from Sri Lanka to Japan, the same phenomenon can be observed: instead of denouncing and stamping out the local gods, the Buddhists have simply converted them to their own cause. People are thus able to continue making use of their traditional religious symbols but within the context of a more highly evolved system of value and meaning. Tibet is no exception to this.

STEPHEN BATCHELOR

Buddhism came to Tibet from India in the seventh century, largely through the endeavors of Trisong Detsen, who invited the great adept Padmasambhava, among others, to bring the Dharma to the people of Tibet. Buddhism subsequently flourished, assimilating aspects of the indigenous Bon religion, until the mid-ninth century, when King Langdarma launched an anti-Buddhist campaign. Buddhism in Tibet entered a dark age as a result, but there was a renaissance in the eleventh century, notably due to the work of the great teacher, Atisha, and that of the former black magician turned yogic adept, Milarepa. Legend has it that the latter survived for years meditating in an isolated cave eating only nettles, and he is often represented in paintings as having a distinctly green color!

Buddhism is frequently categorized into three vehicles: different aspects of Buddhism developed since Buddha's death. Hinayana was the first of these to arise and is still the form practiced in the Theravadan schools of Sri Lanka, Thailand, and Burma. Often, and somewhat misleadingly, called the "lesser" vehicle, it encapsulates the basic teachings of

Above: Japanese monks at the Peace Pagoda in Battersea Park, London

paths require many lifetimes to achieve enlightenment, or Buddhahood, but the tantric practitioner can achieve enlightenment in this very life.

Tibetan Buddhism incorporates both Mahayana and tantra, and comprises four main schools but as the Dalai Lama points out, Mahayana as a development from Hinayana contains the same teachings, and represents the starting point for new practitioners. Much groundwork must be done by studying the sutras – the texts of Buddha's teachings that were written down about five hundred years after his death – and learning basic meditation to develop clarity of mind and single-pointed concentration before moving on to the more advanced tantric practices. As with all quick paths, great care must be taken, and unprepared practitioners might invoke mental disturbances if they have not trained their mind sufficiently first.

One of the underlying impulses to practice Mahayana Buddhism is bodhicitta, the altruistic aspiration to help all living beings reach enlightenment before abiding in nirvana oneself. Such a person is called a bodhisattva.

I try to live my life pursuing what I call the bodhisattva ideal. According to Buddhist thought, a bodhisattva is someone on the path to Buddhahood who dedicates themselves entirely to helping all other sentient beings toward release from suffering. "Bodhi" means the understanding or wisdom of the ultimate nature of reality, and a "sattva" is someone who is motivated by universal compassion. The bodhisattva ideal is thus the aspiration to practice infinite compassion with infinite wisdom.

the historical Buddha. Mahayana was a progression from Hinayana, incorporating particularly the ethical and philosophical developments that occurred in India. Vajrayana, or tantra, can be seen as a further stage, in which symbolism, the idea of transformation, and the use of the body's subtle energies combine in what is known as the "quick path." The other two

Right: Mani stones (engraved with mantras) and chortens, Zanskar

Below: Young monks wearing ceremonial robes and holding drums

Far right: A masked dancer

Right: Prayer flags surrounding the Dalai Lama's residence

Main picture:
Buddha statue
with offering bowls
and butter lamps,
Gyume gompa,
Lhasa, 1994

Above: Lama
Tsong Khapa,
painted on a
rock face

Left: Monks
chanting, Jokhang
temple, Lhasa

TIBETAN BUDDHISM TODAY

Although the Chinese regime in Tibet has now allowed Buddhism to be practiced again, this is limited and controlled. Thus the leading monasteries in India are today the places where the heart of Tibetan Buddhism beats the strongest. A few of the great lamas from Tibet are still alive and teaching there, providing an authentic transmission of Tibetan Buddhism to their younger brethren, many of whom have never seen the country that they identify with. The monasteries have survived well in their new Indian incarnations, but the prosperity that they enjoyed in Tibet has probably gone forever.

Visiting Drepung Loseling Monastery in Mundgod is like walking into another world, which differs from both the West and India. Groups of boisterous young monks look up briefly as you enter, but these days a Western face is not so unusual. One might run up to you carrying a sponsorship form, a sign that the monastery cannot fully support all its residents. The sound of raised voices and clapping hands leads you to the courtyard, where today's debate on the nature of mind is taking place. Even without understanding the language, it is fascinating to stand and watch.

Horns blow loudly, and suddenly everyone is rushing to the main temple for the evening prayer ceremony, and you get caught up in the good-natured but vigorous jostling of the crowd. Inside the temple, brightly colored hangings frame the images of the various deities, some embodying the peace of enlightenment, others in their wrathful aspects frightening away the demons of lust and attachment. The distinctive sound of Tibetan prayers being chanted fills the temple, interspersed with the noise of more horns, cymbals, and thighbone trumpets.

A high lama takes his seat on a raised throne, and smiles out at all the maroon-robed monks, yet does so with a sense of authority that arouses feelings of deep respect. As he starts to teach, the monks quiet down, some scribbling the precious words of wisdom into their scruffy Indian notebooks. If you shut your eyes, the smell of incense fills your senses, and you imagine that you might almost be in Tibet, experiencing Tibetan Buddhism in the land in which it developed.

Main picture: A monk prostrates himself while a fellow monk studies, Bodhgaya, 1973

Left: A typical Tibetan-Buddhist altar, Manali, northern India

Left: A lama holds dice for throwing a mo, a traditional form of divination

10
~

The Four Main Schools
of Tibetan Buddhism

Their seclusion on the Roof of the World enabled the Tibetans to preserve the Mahayana and Tantric

Buddhism of India for over a millennium and to create a uniquely rich spiritual culture.

JOHN SNELLING

Although there are four main schools incorporating various subsects in the Tibetan tradition, they all share a basic theology: Mahayana Buddhist philosophy. As we saw in the previous chapter, Mahayana includes the fundamental teachings of the Hinayana, but has developed to incorporate such ideas as the bodhisattva ideal. Mahayana Buddhism is not confined to Tibet: the Zen Buddhism of Japan and Korea, and the Chinese Ch'an tradition – similar to Zen – are also part of the Mahayana canon. Each school of Buddhism is influenced and conditioned by the culture and indigenous religion of the country within which it has landed, and it is this which gives Tibetan Buddhism its uniqueness.

Although Indian Buddhism has diminished over the centuries, Buddhism's first flowering was in India, where Mahayana thought originated. Some Hinayanists, in their enthusiasm to attain nirvana, dedicated all their energies toward their own libera-

tion and neglected the suffering of the world that they lived in. So it was that a new trend developed, one that emphasized compassion, the wish for all beings no longer to suffer and to find happiness.

I would like to share with my readers a short prayer that gives me great inspiration and determination:
"For as long as space endures,
And for as long as living beings remain,
Until then may I, too, abide
To dispel the misery of the world."

14TH DALAI LAMA

This idea is still central to Tibetan Buddhism today, and the Dalai Lama is regarded as being a human embodiment of Chenrezig, the Buddha of compassion. If you visit Tibet, or the Tibetan communities in exile, you will see the mantra of Chenrezig, "Om Mani Padme Hum," engraved or painted on rocks by the roadside and pathways. A mantra is the symbol in

Left: Windhorses (prayers printed on paper) and incense burning outside the Jokhang temple in Lhasa

sound of the essence of a spiritual ideal, which is also represented visually as a deity or a mandala. You will also become familiar with the sacred sound of this mantra, which Tibetans mutter under their breath as they go about their daily lives, often counting the recitations with prayer beads

Right: The Dalai Lama with the heads of the four main schools of Tibetan Buddhism, India, 1960s

The development of the different schools of Tibetan Buddhism is therefore largely historical, rather than a result of any major doctrinal diversions. All have much in common, and their boundaries are sometimes fluid. It is also often a question of the emphasis of a particular aspect and the adoption of a certain style, that determines a school. Yet each school has its major bodhisattvas and yogic adepts, giving it an individual flavor, and represents an authentic, separate tradition of Tibetan Buddhism.

THE NYINGMA SCHOOL

Nyingma is the oldest of the four traditions, and its origins can be traced back to the first unification of Buddhist tradition in Tibet around the late sixth and early seventh centuries. A legendary figure of that period, Padmasambhava, is credited with introducing

the teachings. The ruler of the time, King Trisong Detsen, invited him and Shantarakshita – a great Indian philosopher – to found a monastery and ordain the first Tibetan monks. Padmasambhava is a partly mythical figure, who has survived in the Tibetan popular imagination by virtue of the magical tales that surround him.

Not born in the usual fashion, Padmasambhava was called the "Lotus Arisen One." Uddiyana, probably located in the Swat Valley in Pakistan, was suffering a terrible drought, so Buddha Amitabha, the Buddha of Infinite Life, spontaneously manifested a beam of red light from his tongue and projected it into the center of a lake, causing a lotus flower to blossom. He then sent the syllable "HRI," a sacred sound, on a beam of light from his heart, which transformed itself into a golden vajra, or scepter, in the center of the lotus. This in turn transformed itself into an eight-year-old boy, who was surrounded by rainbow-like light. The heavens opened, the falling rain ended the drought and so Padmasambhava entered the world.

Many other magical and miraculous tales are told of Padmasambhava's life, as they are of many of the major historical figures of Tibetan Buddhism. Padmasambhava also hid teachings in stones and rocks, and even in the minds of his followers for revelation at a more suitable time. Known as termas, these teachings are still occasionally discovered today. The Nyingma tradition is more inclined to these mythical influences because it is conditioned by Bon (the original, animistic religion of Tibet) than the other traditions.

In recent times, the Nyingma tradition has had many renowned teachers, some of whom have only recently died, such as Kangyur Rinpoche, Dudjom Rinpoche, and Dilgo Khyentse Rinpoche. The

Left: The Dalai Lama and monks wearing the yellow hats of the Gelukpa sect

reincarnations of these great teachers have been iden-
tified and are being educated to fulfill the roles of their
predecessors. In this way, these teachers ensure the
continuity of their tradition. Several Nyingma centers
have opened in France, and one of the major practices
undertaken there is a three-year, three-month, and
three-day retreat, which quite a few Westerners have
successfully completed.

*Right: Sogyal
Rinpoche, one of the
foremost teachers of
Westerners*

Perhaps the best known modern exponent of
Nyingma is Sogyal Rinpoche, who is based in London
but who has centers all around the world. He is the
author of the best-selling work *The Tibetan Book of
Living and Dying*, which is a useful guide for those who
are working with the terminally ill. As a popular book,
it has also introduced many people to Tibetan
Buddhist teachings.

Another prominent lama, Namkhai Norbu
Rinpoche, teaches Dzogchen, a particular teaching of
the Nyingma tradition. Based in Italy, this former
professor of Oriental studies at Naples University has

been the inspiration for others to set up Dzogchen
communities around the world. Translated as "The
Great Perfection," Dzogchen seeks a realization of the
underlying experience of reality.

> *Dzogchen does not see itself as the high point of
> any hierarchy of levels, and is not a gradual
> path... The principal practice of Dzogchen is to
> enter directly into nondual contemplation, and to
> remain in it.*
>
> NAMKHAI NORBU RINPOCHE

Namkhai Norbu Rinpoche is regarded as being
quite unusually innovative by some; however, the spirit
of anarchy is in keeping with this, the oldest of
the Tibetan Buddhist traditions, along with the inclination toward magic and the emphasis on ritual.
Nyingma lamas were often solitary yogis, living in
caves in solitary retreat, or were wandering healers and
teachers. The lamas are not all celibate monks, and
many marry and have children. This tradition also has
a few highly regarded women teachers.

THE SAKYA SCHOOL

The Sakyas enjoyed their heyday several centuries ago,
and though still very much a living tradition of
Tibetan Buddhism, the Sakya school is not now as
prominent as the other three schools. Yet it was
another story in the 1240s, when the Mongol warlord
Prince Godan Khan – Genghis Khan's grandson –
invited Sakya Pandita to teach his people Buddhism.

> *I, the most powerful and prosperous Prince
> Godan, wish to inform the Sakya Pandita, that
> we need a lama to advise my ignorant people on
> how to conduct themselves morally and spiritually*

...As you are the only lama I have chosen, I will not accept any excuse on account of your age or the rigors of the journey.

The request presented in a manner unlikely to generate a refusal, Sakya Pandita accordingly embarked upon the journey to Mongolia. This started the special "priest-patron" relationship between Mongolia and Tibet; softened the most excessive brutalities of Prince Godan and his henchmen; and gave political influence to a monk, thereby unifying religious and political power in Tibet for the first time.

Needless to say, Sakya's ascendancy did not go down well with the other Buddhist schools in Tibet, principally the Kagyus, which had begun at about the same time as the Sakyas in the eleventh century, during the second transmission of Buddhism from India. The link between Tibet and Mongolia strengthened, however, with the succession of Phagpa – the nephew of Sakya Pandita – and also of Kublai Khan – the inheritor of Godan's lands – and this was to last until the present century, though the Sakyas were superseded by the new Geluk tradition in the fourteenth century.

During the period of its ascendancy, the Sakya school had great spiritual influence, as well as political power. One of its major teachings is that of the Triple Vision, which is based on a text by Sachen Kunga Nyingpo, one of the five great Sakya masters who lived during the eleventh century. Drawing from the Lam-dre Hevajra Tantra, the Triple Vision refers to three views of the world: that of an ordinary person; the view of a practitioner who has insight into the true nature of reality; and the totally integrated view of a fully awakened master.

Sakya Trizin, who was born in Tibet in 1945, is currently the 41st spiritual head of the Sakya tradition, and is recognized as an emanation of Manjushri, the enlightened principle of wisdom. Sakya Trizin speaks excellent English and travels and teaches widely, to both Tibetan and Western audiences. In the U.K. there is also a group of Sakya centers that operate under the guidance of Ngakpa Jampa Thaye, a British teacher in this tradition.

Above: The Dalai Lama with Sakya Trizin, head of the Sakya tradition, at the Dalai Lama's residence in Dharamsala

THE KAGYU SCHOOL

"Kagyu" means "transmitted command," and the Kagyus, like the Nyingmas, are more interested in the ritual and mysticism of Buddhism than are the more scholarly Gelukpas. The Kagyu tradition emerged in the eleventh century, and its first leading exponent was Tilopa. Employed as Buddhist teacher to a king, Tilopa felt unfulfilled by his work and eventually escaped, choosing to live in cremation grounds, wearing rags and begging for his food in order to be free to practice meditation. He became renowned as a highly accomplished, but somewhat terrifying, yogic adept.

Tilopa's main disciple was the brilliant scholar Naropa, who had had a vision of a hideous crone who told him that his understanding of Buddhism was only of the words not the meaning, and that he needed to find her brother, Tilopa, to be his teacher. Unable to find this elusive teacher, Naropa was driven to despair and was on the point of taking his life when Tilopa suddenly appeared. He told Naropa that this was a lesson using life situations as a form of teaching rather than trying to find something external. The next lesson was not forthcoming for a year, but Naropa faithfully served his teacher regardless.

Then Tilopa took Naropa to the top of a temple and told him that a true disciple would jump off. Naropa immediately took the plunge and crashed to the ground causing himself great pain. Tilopa next instructed him in tantric practice but subjected Naropa to further "lessons" every year or so. Such stories are common in Tibetan Buddhist tales and imply that all appearances are illusory and that you have to work hard and undergo sometimes painful transformations in order to become enlightened.

Right: The 17th Karmapa, who has been officially accepted by the Chinese government

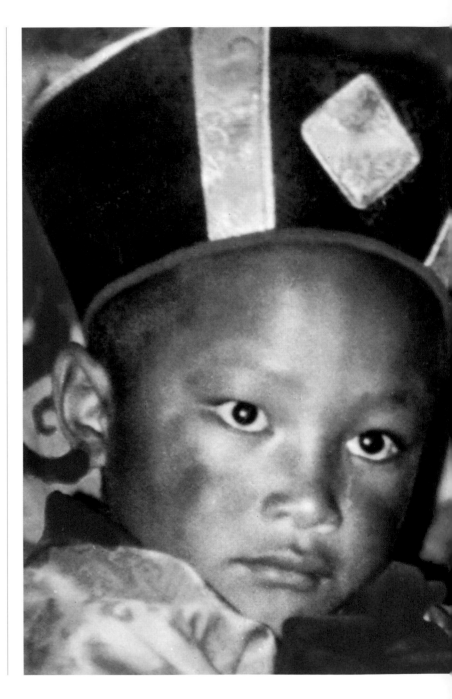

Marpa, a famous translator, was instrumental in bringing the Kagyu teachings to Tibet. His leading disciple was Milarepa, perhaps the most famous of all the Tibetan "saints." A powerful black magician who had killed people, he felt remorse regarding his actions and sought out Marpa. Milarepa underwent terrible hardships to gain the teachings that he wanted, before spending the rest of his life in a remote cave. A highly accomplished meditator, he attracted many disciples and taught others when asked to do so, but he refused to found a monastery or to formalize his teaching in any way.

The Karmapas are the head of the Kagyu school. The present Karmapa, the 17th, is still a boy, the 16th having died in 1981. He has been recognized by the Chinese government, the first time since 1959 that a reincarnated high lama has been formally acknowledged. Ugyen Tinley, at the age of eight, was enthroned at Tsurphu Monastery – the traditional seat of the Karmapas – in Tibet on September 27, 1992.

The first Tibetan Buddhist center in Europe was founded by Chogyam Trungpa Rinpoche and Akong Rinpoche in the Scottish Highlands. A brilliant teacher, who attracted many Western students, Chogyam Trungpa Rinpoche also caused controversy by adopting the counterculture of free sex and psychedelic drugs enjoyed by some of his students. He renounced his monastic vows, married, and went to the United States, where he founded other centers. A mixture of success and scandal surrounded him till he died in 1987, age forty-eight, of an alcohol-related disease. Yet his legacy of important books, such as *Cutting Through Spiritual Materialism,* and flourishing Buddhist centers testify to the fact that despite his unorthodox methods, he had a great deal to offer, although aspects of his lifestyle were perhaps more suited to medieval Tibet.

Like the Nyingmas, the Kagyus have thrived in France, and possibly have more centers in the West than any of the other schools. Samye Ling continues to prosper under Akong Rinpoche. Kalu Rinpoche was another prominent contemporary Kagyu teacher; he died in the 1980s having taught in over forty countries and having established about a hundred centers.

The most important teaching of the Kagyus is Mahamudra, the "Great Symbol," or "Seal," whereby the meditator attempts to realize a natural, relaxed equilibrium.

No matter how confused we might be, there is a dancing ground of experience that is common to everyone ... a basic state of mind that is clear and pure and natural. The realization of that basic state of mind is what is known as Mahamudra.

CHOGYAM TRUNGPA RINPOCHE

Left: Kalu Rinpoche, a prominent contemporary Kagyu teacher

THE GELUK SCHOOL

Geluk translates as "virtuous," and this school was created in the fourteenth century by Je Tsong Khapa, a brilliant and pious monk who wished to restore Tibetan Buddhism to its original purity. Inevitably, the potent combination of religion and politics, along with the passing of centuries, had caused a decline in certain areas of monasticism. Je Tsong Khapa reaffirmed the fundamental importance of following the Vinaya, the original list of rules that had been laid down at the time of the Buddha. He also stressed the necessity of studying the sutras – the sacred texts – as a prerequisite for the more advanced practice of tantra.

Thoroughly versed in the teachings of the existing three schools, Je Tsong Khapa distilled their essence and created a synthesis, resulting in the formation of the new Geluk tradition. He built many monasteries, including Ganden, and also instigated the Monlam, an annual prayer festival held in Lhasa, which survived until the Chinese recently banned it. A brilliant debater, he also corrected some of the doctrinal flaws that had arisen. Although not as colorful and wild as some of the other great Tibetan "saints," Je Tsong Khapa is equally revered for his contribution to Tibetan Buddhism.

He wrote the fundamental teaching of the Gelukpas, the Lam Rim Chenmo – meaning the "Great Exposition of the Graduated Path" – which is commonly known as the "Middle Way." This includes all the preliminary practices of Buddhism, such as developing faith in one's teacher – guru devotion – meditations on impermanence, and the preciousness of having a human rebirth. Detailed study of the hell realms – which are considerably more common than the rare human realm, and look like the nightmarish

Right: Lama Thubten Yeshe, one of the most notable Gelukpa teachers of Westerners, who passed away in 1984

visions of Hieronymus Bosch – remind the practitioner to strive hard toward enlightenment.

This is the most scholarly of the four schools, and a systematic program of studies leading to a Geshe degree is undertaken by those monks who have intellectual ability. Less academically rigorous programs of study exist for the less gifted and for lay people who are unable to dedicate twenty years of their lives to religious study and practice.

The current head of the Gelukpas is Ganden Tri Rinpoche who is democratically elected every seven years. Some Westerners have a particular interest in

Left: Lama Osel on the steps of the Peace Pagoda, London

this school, with a few electing to undertake the strenuous Geshe program, though whether this, in its traditional form, is relevant to Westerners is debatable.

Other than the Dalai Lama – whose main teachings are Gelukpa – the most notable Gelukpa teachers of Westerners include Lama Thubten Yeshe, who died in 1984, and Lama Zopa who is still teaching. Nicknamed the "Inji" (Western) lama, Lama Thubten Yeshe, with his seemingly easy understanding of Western concerns and wonderful, almost showmanlike style, attracted many students. Lama Zopa, a quiet and deeply religious teacher who is famous for his very long teaching sessions, was a perfect teaching companion and they often taught together until Lama Thubten Yeshe died. Lama Yeshe reincarnated as a Spanish boy who is now named Lama Osel, the child of two of his students, and is the first lama to reincarnate as a Westerner.

> As I saw more and more Westerners, I realized they were intellectually advanced. They easily understood the Buddha's teaching. What they lacked, however, was an experience of the teachings which they could only get from meditation.
>
> LAMA THUBTEN YESHE

An offshoot of the Gelukpa school has recently been formed under the leadership of Geshe Kelsang Gyatso, who has called it the New Kadampa tradition. Some controversy has arisen due to a disagreement between the Dalai Lama and Geshe Kelsang Gyatso over the latter's promotion of a protector-deity practice called Dorje Shugden. The Dalai Lama feels that this practice is sectarian and not relevant to modern times, while Geshe Kelsang Gyatso believes that it is important, so this is still practiced by the New Kadampas.

TIBETAN BUDDHIST MEDITATION

As a Buddhist monk and teacher, the Dalai Lama has given hundreds of teachings and discourses on Tibetan Buddhist teachings and meditation. The following advice on why and how to practice meditation has been edited from several teachings.

I always believe the purpose of our life is happiness. There are two kinds, physical comfort and mental peace, and of these two the latter is superior. The reason being, if our mental state is good then if there are some physical problems they can be subdued, but if the mind is restless or uncomfortable then even if a person has the best material facilities he or she still cannot be happy.

Since mental experience is more important than physical experience we need to discover how to train our mind. Human beings are generally quite smart,

not like other animals, and over the centuries we have developed certain techniques to train our mind. These are called meditation. There are two types: analytical meditation, which uses mainly reason; and single-pointed meditation, in which the mind remains focused on one thing. In both cases the main purpose is to gain some control over our mind.

Mental attitude is very important in our daily life. If, when we wake up in the morning, our mind feels happy and fresh then, because the morning mental mood is positive, for the rest of the day some influence will remain and even if we face some problems it is easier to deal with them. But if our mind is unhappy or if we had some nightmare, then even some small problem can easily disturb us.

We cannot buy happiness from the supermarket, like many of the material things we want. Many of today's problems are due to not realizing the importance of basic human values and not taking proper care of our mind; [this is because there is] too much time spent in the supermarket! Therefore meditation is a very important instrument to shape or transform our mind.

TIBETAN BUDDHIST MEDITATION

According to my own little experience as a simple Buddhist monk, I find from my meditation as I get older, even if problems become more serious and responsibility very delicate, my mind is more calm. I hope not from some weakness of body! But from meditation I think my mind is more calm. So problems must be overcome, certainly, but at the same time not much disturbs my peace of mind. This is certainly due to meditation.

With human beings, conflict will always be there. Even within one person, the idea that comes in the morning may be in conflict with the idea that comes in the evening. So even for nonreligious people meditation is useful; it is simply training the mind. Because of human intelligence and discriminating awareness, analytical meditation is more effective. This is a very healthy quality, this skeptical attitude, trying to look for reasons, experimenting, and gaining some experience. In both Buddhism and science the use of reason is essential.

With single-pointed meditation we get less disturbance in our mind, but in the long run there is not much effect; we do not necessarily get a firm conviction this is a good thing. But using both methods together is powerful; if you bring single-pointed awareness to a situation you are analyzing, then this becomes deeper and more forceful. Therefore, we need some experience of single-pointed meditation.

It is best to meditate in the early morning in a quiet place. This is because we train the mind with the mind itself; we do not use external means. Therefore, our mind must be fresh and alert to utilize our best mental state. In the evening we are tired and cannot use our mental faculty properly.

For beginners, first try to withdraw from the external world. Our mind is in our body and should remain there, but our mind has a tendency always to look outside, criticize, and interfere with other things,

not bothered about itself. So now we give it a new instruction and check our mind inside. Sometimes to start with closing the eyes is useful, but the best way is if our eyes are open but not caring what they see.

So we withdraw our eye sense and our ear sense, too. We can make a resolution not to be distracted by our senses going to external objects. Or if they do, making sure our main mind does not follow. Also, we should not get caught up reviewing the past or fantasizing about the future, but remain in the present moment.

We can try to experience some moments of thoughtlessness, some kind of empty feeling like the deep ocean; waves on the surface come and go in the same way that our thoughts arise and pass away, but we do not have to follow them. This is not easy, but it is worthwhile to persevere. Or if this is too difficult, we can start by simply closing our eyes and just have a complete rest. This is not much use in the long run, but it brings some inner calm.

Let the mind flow of its own accord without conceptual overlay. Let the mind rest in its natural state and observe it. In the beginning, when you are not used to this practice, it is quite difficult, but in time the mind appears like clear water. Then stay with this unfabricated mind without allowing concepts to be generated. When we realize this nature of the mind, we can practice analytical meditation.

It is helpful not to practice too long in the beginning and as a result become tired. You should try to meditate for about fifteen minutes, not longer. What is important is the quality of the meditation, not how long the session is. If you meditate for too long you will become sleepy, your mind will become dull; then your meditation will become accustomed to that state. This is not only a waste of time, but is also a habit that is difficult to eliminate in the future.

A sign that your meditative stabilization is progressing well is that even though your meditative session may be long, it will feel as though only a short time has passed. If it seems that you have spent a long time in meditation, even though you have spent only a little, this is a sign that you should shorten the length of the session. This can be very important at the beginning.

11
~

An Introduction to Vajrayana

It would be wrong to deny that some tantric practices do genuinely give rise to mysterious phenomena… Through mental training we have developed techniques to do things which science cannot yet adequately explain.

14TH DALAI LAMA

Main picture: A woman pilgrim turning a hand-held prayer wheel

Below: The hand of Padmasambhava holding a dorje

Vajrayana, or tantra, is sometimes called the "third turning of the wheel of Dharma." The first turning refers to Buddha's teachings and how they were initially interpreted – Hinayana Buddhism. The second refers to the influx of new energy in Buddhism brought about by Mahayana. Vajrayana was also a new trend in Buddhism, but was informed and influenced by the ancient Indian Hindu tantras. At the time that Vajrayana developed, Buddhism in India was on the decline, and there was some debate about whether this was attributable to the advent of tantra, which was seen by some as a degeneration of Buddhism. However, the introduction of Vajrayana into Tibet profoundly inspired and enriched all the schools of Tibetan Buddhism.

Indeed, Tibet was where the term "Vajrayana" was coined, taking its name from the Tibetan symbol of a dorje or vajra, meaning "thunderbolt," which is one of the sacred objects used in the rituals of tantra. There are mythical claims that Buddha Shakyamuni also taught tantra, but, because of its esoteric and powerful nature, limited his audience largely to bodhisattvas, those who were already firmly established on the path to Buddhahood. This raises an important consideration: the practice of Vajrayana is not for the beginner in Buddhist meditation. A person who wishes to practice Vajrayana needs to be well trained in the basic principles of Buddhism, such as morality and compassion; to have reached some understanding of sunyata, the philosophy that all phenomena, including oneself, are empty of inherent existence; and to have trained the mind through meditation.

Having reached this stage, the practitioner now needs to have developed a close relationship with a lama or guru who can first initiate the student into a

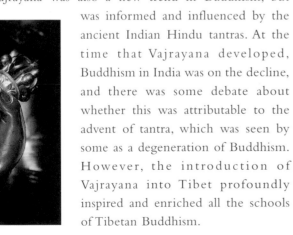

particular tantric practice and then be a spiritual guide. As we have learned already, some teachers seem to behave wildly, and perhaps not in the pious way that we would expect, like Tilopa asking Naropa to jump off a roof. However, tantric teaching states clearly that one must trust one's teacher, not seeing him or her as separate from Buddha. This seems like a tricky dilemma, but the teachings also say that students must choose a teacher over time and examine and be convinced of the teacher's qualities before making a commitment to them.

Why do these teachers behave in such a way? There is a tradition among the Tibetans that some teachers who have become enlightened are not bound by conventional morality and practice what is sometimes called "crazy wisdom."

In tantric Buddhism, the student is required to surrender completely to the teacher and follow his advice unhesitatingly. However unconventional the lama's behavior may be, the student must regard it as the enlightened activity of a Buddha. Hence a disciple would tend not to judge Chogyam Trungpa's alcoholism and sexual profligacy by the standards of ordinary mortals, for she would have been taught to regard them as a display of a mahasiddha's [great yogic adept] transcendent realization.

STEPHEN BATCHELOR

The Dalai Lama has emphasized that students should choose their teachers with great care, and over a period of years. Practicing tantra often requires a commitment to a daily meditational practice, as well as to the guidance of a teacher, so we can see that his advice not to rush into this practice is full of wisdom.

Left: Monks carrying tormas (butter and barley flour molded offerings) and an incense burner

TANTRIC DEITIES

The aim of tantric practice is to transform one's body, speech, and mind into those of a fully enlightened Buddha by special yogic means.

JOHN SNELLING

Nonetheless, practicing Vajrayana is just as authentic and valid a path as any other school of Buddhist meditation. Buddha taught on a variety of different levels to suit the various dispositions of people. From this example we can see that Vajrayana is a path to enlightenment that is suited to some, but not all, aspirants. It is a good idea to ask the advice of a Buddhist teacher whom you know to help you decide whether to enter into this practice, should you have the inclination. But for those who are suited to it, Vajrayana opens the door to a magical and metaphysical realm that is rich in ritual and symbolism.

Another description of Vajrayana is "deity practice." Tibetan Buddhism is rich in deities, some of whom embody the peace and tranquility of enlightenment, as shown by their serene and mysterious smiles. Tara, a female Buddha, is popular, either as Green Tara, with one foot outstretched ready to leap up to help anyone on a spiritual quest, or as White Tara, whose peaceful demeanor symbolizes long life. Such benign deities are perhaps easier to understand and empathize with than those that look like raging, skull-grasping demons bathed in hellfire. Known as wrathful deities they are, however, part of a fully integrated picture.

My first encounter with a host of wrathful deities was in Kalimpong, near the border between India and Bhutan. As I was walking up a long, steep hill, a

monastery came into view, looming high above me in the mist. Somewhat intimidated before I had even gone inside, when I opened the door, I entered a temple covered with floor-to-ceiling wall paintings depicting scenes from various hell realms, as well as every conceivable ferocious protector and deity. I

Below: Tantric practitioner performing mudras with a vajra and bell

wandered around the shrine room casting the occasional glance over my shoulder to ensure nothing was creeping up on me from behind!

Yet in a way something did remain with me from this initial experience. Shortly afterward, I went to Dharamsala, where I encountered Tibetan Buddhism properly and started to practice meditation and mantra recitation. On my return to England, I attended a Tibetan Buddhist center, and several years afterward my teacher encouraged me to be initiated by a high lama who was on a rare visit to the West. I duly followed his advice and, during the initiation ceremony, had a sudden flashback to Kalimpong and the wrathful face of the same deity staring down at me.

So how do these fearsome manifestations fit into a religion that espouses inner peace? This is a common initial confusion until you inquire deeper into Vajrayana. Then you discover a magical and philosophical system of psychological maturity, within which every gesture of a deity means something profound, and every ritual implement held has a special significance. Buddhism encapsulates the idea that the practitioner must use everything that he or she encounters on the path to enlightenment.

This includes all our emotions and psychological states, including the ones that we would normally designate as being negative. Vajrayana does not suppress these feelings or pretend that they do not exist; the practice works by using their raw energy, thereby precluding the value judgments that arise when these emotions are expressed in an unskillful way. The essence of Vajrayana is transformation, and the power behind anger, hatred and so on is utilized by transforming them into their enlightened state. Thus the wrathful deities are the embodiments of these archetypal states of mind, and their vivid depictions are symbolic of the energy that informs them.

States of spiritual attainment are illustrated not by psychological descriptions, but by vibrant personalized gods. By invoking these symbolic figures, the practitioner of the Vajrayana enters into a living relationship and identification with enlightenment as personified by the "deity" with whom he or she has the greatest affinity.

STEPHEN BATCHELOR

TANTRIC PRACTICE

Tantra includes ritual, mantra recitation, and visualization, as well as single-pointed meditation. If you are deemed suitable and ready by your teacher, you then undergo initiation by an appropriately qualified high lama. The initiation involves oral transmission by the teacher to the student, and the teacher can trace his oral transmission in an unbroken lineage back to the great early tantric masters of Tibet. The initiation ceremony may take several hours, or even days, and includes taking vows on morality and often requires a commitment to recite that particular deity's mantra

daily. In some cases, recitation of a scripture – called a sadhana – and performing the visualizations contained therein, is the requirement.

The deity is believed to reside in the center of a mandala, which acts as a spiritual house. Mandalas are pictorially represented as circles within squares within circles, the geometrical forms colored in intricate hues and containing minor deities and protectors. Meditation on a mandala itself helps to transform our level of consciousness, since it symbolizes the transformation of experience that is brought about by enlightenment. During meditation on a mandala, you are drawn into it, and it becomes a three-dimensional sphere.

The deity – known as a yidam, or personal deity, once you have been initiated – has a mantra, which are sacred sounds representing the enlightened speech of a buddha. Once again, mindful recitation of a mantra can help the transformation of consciousness. The sadhana of the deity contains the main mantra, as well as instructions on how to build up a visual image of the deity. Thus the meditation, mantra recitation, and ritual are performed while the practitioner is imagining him- or herself as the deity, together with the enlightened qualities that the deity represents.

The purpose of tantric practice is familiarization; the word "tantra" actually means "continuity," and, by

Below: Tantric implements and hand gestures are an integral part of Vajrayana

Main picture: A monk creates a sand mandala

Right: **Fire puja**
(ceremony) at
Dharamsala

keeping up a daily practice, you can gradually bring about the transformation of your own, as yet unenlightened, consciousness. It does, however, require years of dedicated practice to achieve this.

There are two stages involved in this process of transformation. First it is necessary to rid oneself of conventional ideas and perceptions of who one is and what reality is …The initial practice of the Vajrayana entails systematically familiarizing oneself with this transformed view until it can be sustained in meditation without any distraction for several hours.

STEPHEN BATCHELOR

The first stage to which Batchelor refers is called the generation stage. The second is called the completion stage. During this latter stage, practitioners work with the subtle energies in their bodies, together with their centers and pathways. The centers roughly correspond to the chakras of the central nervous system, and some of the pathways are also utilized in the practice of acupuncture. There is no actual physical reality that is empirically verifiable, yet both the existence of chakras and acupuncture have achieved a level of acceptance in the conventional world. A triumph, perhaps, of mind over matter.

During the second stage, the practitioner visualizes the channels and centers. In most people, they are knotted and intertwined, but by working with the breath and the imagination, the practitioner can free them so that the psychic energies can travel along them unhindered. At death, the channels are freed spontaneously and everyone experiences a state of clear light, although most people pass through unaware of this. The tantric practitioner knows that

this clear light is the fundamental ground of our existence, and therefore endeavors to experience it during meditation. The clear light at death is said to be one of the best opportunities for becoming enlightened, so during meditation the tantric practitioner "practices" what happens psychically at the time of death in order to experience this.

After much practice, the meditator can maintain this experience and the enlightened qualities of the deity while not engaged in meditation, gradually eroding the habitual modes of behavior and thought that keep us caught up in the unsatisfactory confusion of the conventional world. This, then, is the "quick" path of Vajrayana, but it must be stressed that you will require the guidance of a qualified teacher while practicing it, in order not to get lost in the darker realms of your psyche.

Right: Circles within squares within circles are a characteristic feature of a mandala, as in this one from Purne village, Zanskar

VAJRAYANA IN THE WEST

On the positive side, surrender to a lama's authority can serve to undermine egoistic obsessions and open one to a more enlightened perspective on life. If the lama is able to direct the student to spiritual freedom and understanding, then the relationship can result in the recovery and enhancement of one's own inner authority. But, as the Tibetan texts emphasize, utmost care and discretion must precede such an intimate commitment. If not, at best confusion and at worst exploitation will result.

STEPHEN BATCHELOR

As the number of Tibetan Buddhist centers in the West proliferated during the 1970s – largely due to the interest of those Western students who had first encountered Tibetan Buddhism in India – attraction to the more esoteric practices developed. The cultural gap between Asia and the West became evident in the different interpretations of the "long time" that it takes to achieve enlightenment, and comparatively new students wanted to join their more experienced fellow practitioners in these secret and colorful practices.

The lamas were impressed by the psychological maturity that Western culture developed in many of its people and were pleased with the desire expressed by their students to undertake serious meditational practices. However, they were perhaps not fully conversant with the equally Western habit of trying out new things and then moving on when the next exciting adventure comes into view. They were also a little puzzled by the emotional instability that was displayed by some of the people who were attracted to Buddhism. For those with a healthy ego, a philosophy

that reduces attachment to it is helpful, but for some of the more insecure students, it merely served to increase their neuroses.

At first, many centers requested high lamas to perform initiations. Initiations duly occurred, along with students' daily commitments to practice. But these new circumstances meant the high lama was no longer available following the initiation to maintain a close relationship with the students in the traditional manner because they returned to their monasteries shortly after. Some students practiced for a while, became bored or tired, or experienced a life crisis and simply stopped, regardless of the commitments that they had made. Others developed psychological problems in conjunction with their practice. Some students were fine, however, and continue their tantric practice to this day, finding it rewarding and beneficial.

The lamas then realized that for many Westerners, Vajrayana – or the commitment to daily practice – was inappropriate. Now there are fewer initiations, and those that are given are often done so on the simpler level of a blessing, with the option of daily practice. However, for the experienced Western student of Tibetan Buddhism, who has a good relationship with a lama at a nearby center, Vajrayana is still a valuable option.

Having myself maintained a daily practice for about ten years, I have found it a mixed blessing. I experienced some psychological turbulence during the first few years, and since the initiating lama had returned to India, he was not at hand to give advice. Some support was offered by my teacher at the center, but he later became quite ill and thus also became unavailable to help. Others, mainly experienced Western teachers and fellow practitioners, have offered me guidance and support over the years. On reflection,

Left: A practitioner of tantra with traditional ritual implements of bell and drum

I am happy to have this daily practice, but sometimes it has been a struggle to maintain. I am still very much a beginner in my practice of Vajrayana but have observed some benefits nonetheless.

In the praises of wrathful deities it is always mentioned that they do not stir from the Truth Body or from love. If a practitioner of tantra who did not have the prerequisite of the development of strong compassion attempted such wrathful practice, it would harm rather than help ... It is extremely important to have the prerequisites and all qualifications for the practice of tantra.

14TH DALAI LAMA

12
~
Tibetan Buddhism
in the West

The essence of the Buddhist teachings does not change; wherever it goes it is suitable.
However, the superficial aspects – certain rituals and ceremonies – are not necessarily suitable for
a new environment and those things will change. How they will change in a particular place
we cannot say; this evolves over time.

14TH DALAI LAMA

mong the hippies and travelers heading East in the 1960s were some who would change irrevocably before their return home around a decade later. Their collective spirit

embraced the cultures of these foreign lands, partly because they were exotic; but a fascination with religions lived as an integral part of daily life also played a significant role.

Some people are more fond of one food; others find
another more suitable. Similarly, for some
individuals a certain religion brings more benefit,
whereas in other cases another brings more benefit.
Under the circumstances, the variety of teachings
found in human society is necessary and useful, and
among Westerners, no doubt there are people who
find Buddhism suitable to their requirements.

14TH DALAI LAMA

The overland trail through Turkey, Iran, Pakistan, and Afghanistan often culminated in India where Hindus, Muslims, Catholics, and Jains lived side by side

Main picture:
The Dalai Lama
greeting the
welcoming party at
Lam Rim Buddhist
Centre, Wales, in
1996

Left: Early Western
Buddhist students,
Dharamsala, 1970

in a cultural mix like a fantasy from *The Arabian Nights.* When the intense heat of the early Indian summer drove the Westerners up to the mountains, some arrived in Dharamsala, where they encountered Tibetan Buddhism. For many, this was just another colorful spectacle, to be enjoyed at the time and then moved on from as easily as it had been met, generally when the monsoon made living conditions less idyllic. But for a few, the impact of this way of life proved profound and transformed their lives forever.

Some people went to Nepal, mainly in and around Kathmandu, where there was another Tibetan Buddhist community intermingled with that of the Nepalese, whose own religion was influenced by the Buddhism of their neighbor, Tibet. Some of these travelers, who were not seduced by the wide range of

Below: A Westerner standing beside the Durga temple (Hindu), Dharamsala

recreational drugs available in Kathmandu, also found Tibetan Buddhism to their taste. Thus it was that another community of Westerners immersed in Tibetan Buddhism and culture evolved.

Of course, the 1960s was not the first encounter between Western and Buddhist cultures. Over the centuries, a few pioneering travelers and dedicated scholars had followed the same trail, though in a less flamboyant way, and had returned to write books detailing their experiences and research. But these works remained mainly in esoteric libraries, read only by a handful of people. This time, Tibetan Buddhism and culture, along with those of Hinduism and Islam, influenced the alternative, but popular, youth culture and tapped into the imagination of many people.

The young, often idealistic, travelers who stayed in Dharamsala found in the Tibetans a people who shared some of their beliefs, albeit in a different cultural context. A desire for peace and love was common, and with the anti-Vietnam War demonstrations of recent memory, the Westerners felt a real empathy with the displaced Tibetan people, as well as respect for their fundamental belief in the use of nonviolent methods to solve their problems.

The idea of transforming one's consciousness was also not new to either community, though the mediums used in order to achieve this were very different. Many of the hippies had experimented with hallucinogenic drugs, and smoking marijuana was common; thus they already had a good idea that the mind's perception of reality was variable. They were therefore often attracted to the safer and slower path of meditation, preferring to search for these experiences within themselves rather than simply relying on external substances.

So, throughout the late 1960s and the 1970s a community of Westerners slowly grew among the Tibetans in McLeod Ganj, and in the surrounding small villages and isolated huts in the hills. Courses in meditation and Tibetan Buddhist philosophy that were specifically designed for Westerners were established – also in Kathmandu – and, after a few initial hiccups, began to flourish. Serious students sought out some of the highest lamas and requested teachings, which these teachers, who often lived simply and, at that time, accessibly, were happy to provide. Some students even became ordained, and Westerners dressed in Tibetan robes became a familiar sight in the community.

THE RETURN HOME

When Buddhism first came from India to Tibet, no one had the authority to say "Now Buddhism has come to a new land; from now on we must practice it in this way or that way." There was no such decision. It gradually evolved, and in time a unique tradition arose. Such may be the case for Westerners; gradually in time there may be a Buddhism combined with Western culture. In any case, this generation – your generation – who are starting this new idea in new countries has a big responsibility to take the essence and adjust it to your own environment.

14TH DALAI LAMA

Living in Asia is as exacting on the body as it is refreshing to the mind when one is accustomed to a Western lifestyle, and almost all those who lived there suffered illnesses, ranging from mild digestive upsets to the sometimes fatal hepatitis. Inevitably, this began to influence some of the Westerners in India and Nepal

and contributed to their natural desire to return home for longer than a brief visit every few years following a decade or so away. Such feelings were mixed, however; what had attracted these people to their adopted culture had not changed, and some wished to stay there indefinitely.

Meanwhile, the Indian government was not oblivious to the presence of these Western settlers, and in the early 1980s decided to upgrade its tourist policy.

Above: A Westerner wearing ceremonial dress and participating in a fire puja, Drepung Monastery, southern India

It was desirous of welcoming rich visitors who would go home after two weeks of sightseeing, rather than backpackers on low budgets, or people who slotted into local economies without bringing in much foreign money. Not all the foreigners who chose to live in India were like the responsible majority of those in Dharamsala, and the Indians were also tired of repatriating heroin addicts and other undesirables who had run out of money.

Below: Lama Yeshe's cremation ceremony is attended by his Western students, Vajrapani Institute,

Along with requiring British visitors to have visas for the first time in 1984, the government staged local clean-up operations in all the areas where Westerners were known to reside. Dharamsala was no exception, and by 1985 the majority of those Westerners who had lived there for over a decade were headed home, back to Europe and the United States. Although it had been enforced by the Indian authorities, their return home was a natural process, prompted also by the desire to share the wisdom that they had learned from Tibetan Buddhism with their fellow countrymen in the West.

TEACHING TIBETAN BUDDHISM IN THE WEST

An interesting phenomenon of the past two decades or so has been the rapid growth of interest in Buddhism among Western nations … I am always glad if someone derives benefit from adopting Buddhist practices. However, when it actually comes to people changing their religion, I usually advise them to think the matter through very carefully. Rushing into a new religion can give rise to mental conflict and is nearly always difficult.

14TH DALAI LAMA

Among the first wave of Westerners who had encountered Tibetan Buddhism abroad were those who had chosen not to live there for more than a year or two, or only to visit it for a few months each year. A few of these people had already initiated the establishment of Dharma centers and had brought Tibetan lamas to the West to teach and be the spiritual heads of these centers. Such establishments began to attract plenty of students who had been neither to India nor

Nepal and had not encountered Tibetan culture, but who were deeply impressed with the teachings of Tibetan Buddhism.

There inevitably arose cultural misunderstandings, ranging from problems caused by bad English translations of Tibetan texts to the unfulfilled expectations of both the Tibetan teachers and their students. Such problems did not adversely affect the majority, but nonetheless, the difficulties of individuals could affect the mood of a group. It became obvious that the direct and unmodified transposition of Tibetan Buddhism to students in the West needed to be more integrated, at least for some of the students.

Thus arose the phenomenon of Western teachers of Tibetan Buddhism. Such positions provided useful and authentic roles for the most learned of the long-term students who wished to teach, some of whom had recently returned from their immersion in Tibetan culture in India. The Western teachers did not supplant the Tibetan lamas in any way; this was never the intention. What they did provide, however, was an understanding of the psychological issues affecting the often young, Western students who were attracted to Tibetan Buddhism that had not always been addressed by the Tibetan lamas.

Although Tibetan Buddhism attracted students who were genuinely interested in what the teachings had to offer, and how they could thereby enhance their lives, it also brought some people who were psychologically damaged, or society's outcasts. These people were often looking for salvation from their dilemmas in something different and benign, but their expectations of what Tibetan Buddhism could provide were unrealistic. This caused individual disappointment and sometimes disruption within the centers.

Thus the experienced Western-students-turned-teachers were confronted with some tricky and sensitive problems while running their courses in basic Tibetan Buddhism and meditation. It became clear that although Buddhism ultimately does provide a fully integrated spiritual path leading to enlightenment, some people need to experience other techniques and methods before embarking on such a path. Therefore, the different traditions of psychotherapy began to play a role.

Some students of Buddhism had naturally become interested in psychotherapy, for this can be a spiritual path in itself, and had undertaken various trainings in transpersonal psychotherapy, psychosynthesis, Gestalt, psychology, and so on. Working with both Buddhist teachings and psychotherapy over the years proved useful in dealing with the problematic students of Buddhism, as well as helping to design courses in Buddhist teachings and meditation retreats.

Above: Namkhai Norbu with a group of Western students visiting Tibet

TIBETAN BUDDHISM AND OTHER BUDDHIST TRADITIONS

Also among Buddhists, there are different schools, different systems of practice, and we should not feel that one teaching is better, another teaching is worse, and so on. Sectarian feeling and criticism of other teachings or other sects is very bad, poisonous, and should be avoided.

14TH DALAI LAMA

Right: Western students on a trip to Tibet with Lama Zopa Rinpoche

As well as exploring Western psychotherapy, some students of Tibetan Buddhism had practiced Vipassana from the Burmese, Sri Lankan, and Thai traditions, as well as the Korean and Japanese Zen traditions. They found that the different techniques could work together harmoniously, and so they began to be incorporated into some of the courses run in the United States and Europe. This synthesis is reflected in a Western-Buddhist tradition that also draws on Western philosophy, founded by Sangharakshita in 1967 and called the Friends of the Western Buddhist Order.

These different approaches suit different people and some students and teachers strongly feel that practicing one tradition purely is appropriate for them; while others find that exploring a synthesis of traditions will slowly lead toward a Western Buddhism that arises organically and draws what is useful from all traditions. These different schools of Buddhism generally coexist in a spirit of tolerance and welcome the opportunity for discussion and practice together, without thereby invalidating the purity of each tradition and approach.

Tibetan Buddhism, with its own four schools, flourishes in this broader Buddhist context. Many centers practice purely within their tradition, while

many other courses and retreats use Tibetan Buddhist teachings alongside Vipassana and psychotherapy. With the occasional exception, the spirit of tolerance encapsulated in the Buddhist teachings prevails, and Tibetan Buddhism enriches the lives of many Westerners today.

TIBETAN BUDDHISM IN THE WEST TODAY

The most important thing is practice in daily life; then you can know gradually the true value of religion ... I hope that you engage in practice with a good heart and from that motivation contribute something good to Western society. That is my prayer and wish.

14TH DALAI LAMA

The spirit of Tibetan Buddhism is thriving and growing stronger in the West all the time. Any attempt to quantify it in terms of numbers of centers is doomed to a swift obsolescence; sufficient to say that there are over a thousand centers – big and small – throughout the Western world today. What is perhaps more interesting is to trace the evolution of a couple different centers from their spontaneous beginnings, when they sprouted from the enthusiasm of Tibetan lamas and their students.

Jamyang – a center in the Gelukpa tradition – was originally called Manjushri, because it was associated with the already existing Manjushri Centre in Cumbria, England. The original Manjushri is now the headquarters of the New Kadampa tradition, and when this became incompatible with the younger London center it was transformed into the Jamyang Meditation Centre. Originally the center was not a physical building, and from 1979 meetings between

*Right: Western
monks and nuns
in prayer at Samye
Ling Tibetan
Centre, Scotland*

interested people occurred in various apartments, the disused Cambodian Embassy, and a room in the Buddhist Society building.

The inspiration for this London center came from Lama Yeshe, Geshe Kelsang, and Lama Zopa, who all visited and taught regularly in London. Eventually, in 1982, a house in the Finsbury Park area of north London was purchased and converted into London's first official Gelukpa Buddhist center. A lama, Geshe Wangchen, soon took up residence and the student numbers grew till the gompa, or shrine room, was packed on the nights on which Geshela, as he was familiarly called, taught.

A visiting high lama would occasionally come and give teachings and initiations. During the late 1980s, Geshe Wangchen became seriously ill and was therefore absent from the center for long periods of time; eventually, he returned to India for health reasons. Meanwhile, an American monk, John Feuille, came and taught in the absence of a resident lama, along with visiting Tibetan lamas and other Western monks and nuns. Geshe Tashi arrived in the early 1990s and became the resident teacher, assisted by John and other senior students.

At this point, it became necessary to look for larger premises, since the house in Finsbury Park could no longer contain the growing number of students coming for teachings. So, on the advice of Lama Zopa, who was still the spiritual head of the center, the dedicated students made a huge and successful fundraising effort and bought an old courthouse in south London. This was in a dilapidated condition and needed a lot of building and conversion work, therefore a year or two of intense physical effort began, largely carried out by volunteers.

Today, Jamyang is a well attended center, running a regular program of classes ranging from basic meditation to more advanced Buddhist philosophy. Some of the old faces can still be seen; many new people also now attend once or twice a week and come for the events that Jamyang holds on the days of the major Tibetan Buddhist festivals.

In 1986, Jewel Heart was founded in Ann Arbor, Michigan, and continues to sponsor public talks, meditational instruction and practice, courses in Tibetan Buddhism, and retreats on various practices and teachings. Kyabje Gelek Rinpoche is the spiritual director of this center; he is related to the family of the 13th Dalai Lama. Kyabje Gelek Rinpoche studied at Drepung with both the senior and junior tutors of the 14th Dalai Lama, and fled into exile in 1959. After spending several years in India, he moved to the United States.

Kyabje Gelek Rinpoche is fluent in English, and has become accustomed to popular Western culture with astonishing ease; he is, therefore, ideally suited to teach Westerners. His main aim is to make traditional Buddhist training practical and accessible to contemporary practitioners. He has recently taken U.S. citizenship and draws on examples from American culture and politics to inform his teaching sessions.

There is a structured program for students, which is also followed at associated centers or chapters in other cities. These include weekly and monthly study courses and two one-week retreats each year, the latter bringing together many students in the United States, as well as from centers in Holland, Malaysia, and Singapore. During meditational retreats there are courses available in thangka painting, talks by visiting lamas, as well as by Kyabje Gelek Rinpoche, and there

Far right:
Chenrezig painting
by Peter Iseli

Below: Lama
Zopa at the Peace
Pagoda, London

were poetry readings by the late Allen Ginsberg, who was a Jewel Heart board member.

In April, 1994, Jewel Heart board members and students were thrilled to sponsor a visit by the Dalai Lama to Ann Arbor. Events, held at the University of Michigan, included a public talk by the Dalai Lama, a Tibetan cultural festival with displays of Tibetan folk

art and ritual objects, and a piano recital by the renowned modern composer Philip Glass, who is on the Jewel Heart board.

The United States has approximately four hundred centers these days, ranging from the very small, with just a few members and affiliated with a monastery or particular teacher, to the very large, such as the many retreat centers. Some long-term, experienced teachers in the United States, such as Geshe Michael Roach and Ven. Thubten Chodron (formerly Cherry Green) are working toward establishing pure traditions of Tibetan Buddhism in the United States. Four years ago, Geshe Michael had only a handful of students in his classes, but now they number over sixty. This interest is reflected in many countries around the world today, and new centers are blossoming.

Thus each center has a unique story and flavor, depending on the country in which it is based and which Tibetan school it follows, but the development from small, enthusiastic informal groups meeting in people's homes to buildings designed specifically for the purpose of spiritual practice is common. Often facing seemingly insurmountable financial problems, the centers find sponsors who make the dream of a new shrine room, or a larger building, come true. Much is achieved by students who volunteer their time freely to make these centers function so that the precious teachings of Tibetan Buddhism are available to all those who walk through the door.

This spirit of giving is fundamental to Buddhist teachings and is also reflected in various activities undertaken by some of the students. These include taking food to the homeless in most of the large cities, and sending old clothes to some of the poorest communities in India. Sometimes, trusts are set up

specifically for these purposes, like Rokpa, which functions internationally. Such actions, perhaps more than any number of centers, indicate that Buddhism has arrived in the West and that it has become integrated with the traditional Christian spirit of giving in our own Western cultures.

What will happen to Tibetan Buddhism in its country of origin, in the Tibetan communities in exile, and in its new phase in the West remains unknown. And Buddhism in the West is not always a success story.

> *I have met Westerners who at the beginning were very enthusiastic about their practice, but after a few years have completely forgotten it, and there are no traces of what they had practiced at one time. This is because at the beginning they expected too much.*
>
> 14TH DALAI LAMA

Yet Tibetan Buddhism in the West is here to stay, although it is likely to remain peripheral to mainstream society, even as the number of people calling themselves Buddhists grows, as well as the centers that some of them attend. The teachings of the Buddha – the Dharma – are ultimately concerned with relieving the suffering of existence, and how Tibetan Buddhism contributes to this in the West is its measure as an authentic, living Buddhist tradition.

> *The practice of the Dharma is only meaningful if a significant transformation is effected within the practitioner. As long as the practitioner remains unaffected, the Dharma can be no more than a consolation, a diversion, a fascination, or an obsession… The person and the practice are not two different things.*
>
> STEPHEN BATCHELOR

Compassion: Our Universal Responsibility

The Dalai Lama frequently stresses the importance of universal responsibility for each person, whether or not this is practiced in the context of a religion. Compassion is the spontaneous response to dissatisfaction and suffering, and together with universal responsibility is a good way to find peace. The following extracts are taken from the Dalai Lama's public talks over a period of years.

When you see humanity facing certain problems, mainly manmade problems, then in order to solve these problems I believe the best way is through human understanding, which is based upon fundamental human feeling. Now, if we look closely at the nature of humanity, from birth till death, affection and compassion are the most important feelings of a human being. Without these, humanity cannot survive. So, therefore, under such circumstances, I always believe it is very important to have a sense of universal responsibility on the basis of compassion, love, and forgiveness.

Compassion means not only feelings of pity or sympathy; compassion is, I think, the genuine concern about others. So you see, with compassion our sense of responsibility will develop and increase. Also, I think, it is very important to know that the practice of love and compassion is not mainly a religious matter. Now religion is very good, but sometimes I think religion and moral ethics are a luxury. Even without religion we can manage, we can survive. But compassion and love – without these things we cannot survive.

Everyone, irrespective of cultural background, faith, and social circumstances, by nature has the feeling of "I." With that feeling of "I" also comes the desire to achieve happiness and overcome suffering. That feeling is there right from the beginning of human life on this planet. This feeling determines the entire human development and history. This will never change, whatever material or technological advances occur.

You must first realize this from your own experience. If someone looks at you with a smile, with affection, you will feel happy; if someone scowls, you will feel uncomfortable. You will then know that other people are also human beings, and also want love and compassion. Thus, to create reliable friends you need love, compassion, sincerity, and openness.

Today, due to the development of science and technology, our destructive power is now immense and at a real danger point. Under such circumstances I think the realization of the oneness of an entire human being is the same as the oneness of every human being. I think this is important. So I feel love and kindness is something like a universal religion. You may be an antireligious person, but you still need loving kindness.

One old scientist I met, a brain specialist, told me that while a child is in its mother's womb, the mother's mental peace is very important. Also that simply touching the body of her child is the most important factor for the healthy development of the child's brain. This shows humanity really needs affection.

Sometimes there is conflict between short- and long-term attitudes, but for the sake of our planet it is very important we take the long-term view. In our

Top left:
A Christian nun
attends the Dalai
Lama's teachings,
Dharamsala, 1997

Above: A nun
studying at Ganden
Choeling nunnery.

Left: Tibetan
children in a village
near Lhasa

Far left:
A monk hands out
blessing strings at
the Dalai Lama's
public audience

global crisis we can't blame a few politicians; entire humanity, every human being, has responsibility. Thus we need a sense of universal responsibility.

So, brothers and sisters, if you agree with some of these thoughts then try to implement them yourself and explain them to others. But if you feel they are not much use to humanity, then there is no problem, you can just forget them.

✢

I feel that for young people it is easier to express feelings. There is more honesty. When we get older there are more circumstances and conditions; things are not so clear. So in that respect our young people, the new generation, are a key force. I feel really encouraged that so many young people are trying to implement the idea of a nonviolent and compassionate society.

The next century I hope will be one of dialog and not of killing. This twentieth century has perhaps been the worst for killing and bloodshed through human action. We experimented with violence and war as a way to solve our problems, but we failed. If we exchange the money used on armaments for more constructive, peaceful methods then there will be much benefit.

Dialog is a more constructive way, and we see some start of this now. Disagreement and conflict will always be there, because of human beings; if our planet had no human beings it would be a safer place. But no one wants to die! And we are already here. Humans also have great potential for good, and through combining intelligence and good heart, altruism can develop. Other animals cannot do this; this is our unique quality. So we should recognize this as a good thing and use it effectively.

✢

Compassion is the source of nonviolent action, and it brings us inner strength and mental peace. With these qualities compassion also brings us more smiles, friendship, and harmony. So compassion is really something very precious. It opens our inner doors and allows us to communicate with other fellow human beings more easily and even [with] animals. So we develop genuine friendship and reduce our sense of insecurity and fear, and develop self-confidence, which bring us more inner strength and peace.

There is also less chance of developing hatred, anger, and jealousy. These disturb our peace of mind, and if you keep them inside, this closes our inner doors automatically and makes it difficult to communicate with others, and destroys our inner peace and health. There is a common misperception in thinking that anger is our protector and gives us extra energy, but if we look more carefully, the energy brought by anger is blind. It is best, therefore, to know these afflictive emotions are harmful, and this helps prevent them from arising.

✢

Right: A young Tibetan mother with her child

Top left: Tibetan schoolchildren with hands folded in a gesture of respect and greeting; one holds a picture of the Dalai Lama

Above: Elderly Tibetan women spinning prayer wheels, Mundgod, southern India

Left: Tibetan women in Dharamsala holding malas, incense, and katas, waiting to see the Dalai Lama

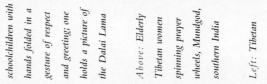

GLOSSARY OF BUDDHIST TERMS

Bodhicitta: the altruistic mind that aspires to attain enlightenment in order to help all beings find happiness

Bodhisattva: someone on the path to enlightenment who has generated bodhicitta

Buddha: an enlightened being; the first of the Three Jewels

Buddha Shakyamuni: the historical Buddha, Siddhartha Gautama

Buddhadharma: literally the teachings of the Buddha

Chakra: literally circle; an energy or psychic nerve center in the body

Compassion: the wish to free all beings from suffering

Conventional truth: also relative truth; the way things appear to those who are not yet enlightened and unable to perceive ultimate truth, i.e. not perceiving phenomena as they really exist

Deity: a Buddha represented in a symbolic form, peaceful or wrathful

Deity practice: a form of tantric practice using meditation, mantra, and visualization on a particular deity, known as a yidam, or personal deity, once someone has been initiated into the practice

Dharma: can mean several things, but here it is used to mean the word of the Buddha, the Buddha's teachings, and the second of the Three Jewels

Geluk/Gelukpa: also Gelug; one of the four main schools of Tibetan Buddhism

Geshe: an honorific title, usually for a monk in the Geluk tradition who has undergone a systematic course of study and retreat and passed a final examination qualifying the person to teach Tibetan Buddhism

Guru: spiritual teacher or master

Hinayana: literally, but somewhat misleadingly, lesser vehicle. The path

followed by Buddhist traditions that try to realize enlightenment for the individual, but also the basis for Mahayana Buddhism

Karma: the actions of our body, speech, and mind. Whether good or bad, they are motivated by unenlightened delusion and serve as the cause for future rebirth – good actions cause good rebirth and vice versa, but karma operates over many lifetimes, and conditions must be appropriate for karma to ripen, thus it is more complex than simple cause and effect

Kagyu: one of the four main schools of Tibetan Buddhism

Lama: spiritual teacher or guru, not always a geshe

Mahayana: literally greater vehicle, the Buddhist path that tries to realize enlightenment for the benefit of all beings

Mantra: sacred syllables, usually repeated many times as part of spiritual practice

Meditation: there are two principal types in Tibetan Buddhism, analytical and single-pointed concentration. Both train the mind and work toward transformation of consciousness to attain enlightenment

Mo: divination by saying prayers and throwing dice

Nectar: a divine offering to the Buddha(s), usually visualized or substituted by tea or alcohol in ceremonies. It is said that an enlightened being or Buddha can transform impure substances into nectar

Nyingma: one of the four main schools of Tibetan Buddhism

Oracle: a person acting as a medium for a protector spirit who manifests after the medium has dressed in ceremonial robes and headdress and entered a trance

Protector: a wrathful deity that helps to protect a person or country from those with bad intentions

Reincarnation: the most subtle level of

consciousness together with the karma accrued by the previous incarnations that pass from one lifetime to the next

Rinpoche: literally precious one, used by Tibetans to designate respect for a reincarnate lama who when young is also known as a tulku

Sadhana: a religious text or scripture detailing a tantric practice and including instructions on saying mantras, visualization, and the recitation of prayers and praises

Samsara: literally cyclic existence, continuously being born and dying and being reborn again before a person achieves enlightenment and enters nirvana

Sangha: the spiritual community, our spiritual friends, sometimes used to mean monks and nuns only, the third of the Three Jewels

Sunyata: literally emptiness or voidness, a philosophy believing that all things are empty of inherent existence, i.e. they cannot exist alone, but depend upon their constituent parts and environment

Stupa: a religious monument in a particular style and shape, but any size, symbolizing Buddha's inner qualities

Sutra: the teachings of the Buddha, spoken or written

Tantra or tantrayana: also called vajrayana, literally continuity, usually meaning deity practice that aims to transform a person's body, speech, and mind into those of a Buddha

Three Jewels: Buddha, Dharma, and Sangha, all a person needs to rely on, or take refuge in, to reach enlightenment

Tulku: *see* Rinpoche

Ultimate Truth: the way things really are, i.e. empty of inherent existence and interdependent on their constituent parts and environment

Vajrayana: *see* Tantra

BIBLIOGRAPHY

Books

Avedon, John F., *In Exile from the Land of Snows* (Wisdom Publications, 1985)

Batchelor, Stephen, *The Awakening of the West* (Aquarian, 1994)

Batchelor, Stephen, *The Tibet Guide* (2nd edition, Wisdom Publications, 1998)

Bell, Sir Charles, *Portrait of a Lama: The Life and Times of the Great Thirteenth* (Wisdom Publications, 1987)

Gyatso, Tenzin (14th Dalai Lama), *A Policy of Kindness* (Snow Lion Publications, 1993)

Gyatso, Tenzin (14th Dalai Lama), *Freedom in Exile* (Abacus, 1992)

Gyatso, Tenzin (14th Dalai Lama), *Kindness, Clarity, and Insight* (Snow Lion Publications, 1984)

Norbu, Thubten Jigme and Turnbull, Colin, *Tibet: Its History, Religion and People* (Pelican Books, 1972)

Snelling, John, *The Elements of Buddhism* (Element Books, 1990)

Journals

Shambhala Sun, Volume 5, Number 2 (November 1996, Boulder)

Videos

A Man of Peace (The Meridian Trust and The Tibet Office of Information and International Relations, London, 1989)

Contribution of the Individual to World Peace (The Meridian Trust, London, 1984)

In the Presence of Compassion: H.H. The Dalai Lama's UK Visit 1993 (The Meridian Trust, London, 1993)

In the Spirit of Free Enquiry (The Meridian Trust, London 1993)

Peace in Action: H.H. The Dalai Lama's UK Visit 1996 (The Meridian Trust, London, 1996)

Secular Meditation (The Foundation for Universal Responsibility, Delhi, 1995)

The Last Resort (Majo Film, Denmark, 1991)

PICTURE ACKNOWLEDGMENTS

INDEX